TO GOD'S GLORY

Lessons on Puritanism

Joel R. Beeke and Nicholas J. Thompson

REFORMATION HERITAGE BOOKS

Grand Rapids, Michigan

To God's Glory
© 2019 by Joel R. Beeke and Nicholas J. Thompson

Reformation Heritage Books
3070 29th St. SE
Grand Rapids, MI 49512
616-977-0889
orders@heritagebooks.org
www.heritagebooks.org

Printed in the United States of America
21 22 23 24 25 26/10 9 8 7 6 5 4 3 2

ISBN 978-1-60178-655-5

For additional Reformed literature, request a free book list from Reformation Heritage Books at the above regular or e-mail address.

TABLE OF CONTENTS

INTRODUCTION

What is Puritanism?

Just what is meant by the term *Puritan*? The word was first used in the 1560s of those English Protestants who considered the reforms under Queen Elizabeth incomplete and called for further "purification" in the Church. It originally had a negative connotation, used by those who were less than appreciative of these English reformation-minded ministers. But the term Puritanism was quickly embraced as a positive description of the reform movement which sought to bring the Church of England into greater conformity to the Word of God.

There were three main areas in which the Puritans pursued reformation. First, in the pulpit. They advocated for biblically and doctrinally sound preaching of the Word. Second, in the people. They stressed the need of personal godliness and the work of God's Spirit. Third, in the manner of worship. They promoted simplicity in liturgy, vestments, and church government.

The Puritans experienced some success for a time in achieving this goal of reformation. In 1662, however, the Act of Uniformity was passed which required all ministers to give public assent to the use of the Book of Common Prayer and to use it exclusively. Most Puritan ministers could not submit themselves in good conscience to this since they viewed the English prayer book as a middle way between Roman Catholic and Reformation teaching. This led to what became known as the great ejection where more than two thousand ministers were expelled from their churches and home, and deprived of their incomes because they would not conform to the use of the Book of Common Prayer as the uniform order for worship in the Church of England. But there were some Puritans who sought to reform the Church of England from within, remaining as long as they were granted the freedom to preach.

In this way, Puritanism encompasses those in England and North America who, from the reign of Elizabeth I until the beginning of the eighteenth century, worked to reform and purify the church and to lead people toward godly living consistent with the Reformed doctrines of grace. As will be seen in the subsequent lessons, it was by no means a monolithic movement. Yet, for the most part, there was a remarkable unity of thought, conviction, and experience among the Puritans.

Why Study the Puritans?

Maybe you are thinking, why so much focus on the Puritans? While these English ministers were far from perfect, there is much that we today can learn from their lives and writings. Here are five characteristics that permeate Puritan thought and account for their continuing relevance and power.

1. The Puritans viewed life in light of Scripture. They loved, lived, and breathed Scripture, regarding the sixty-six books of the Bible as the library of the Holy Spirit graciously bequeathed to Christians. They called believers to be Word-centered in faith and practice. Henry Smith said, "We should set the Word of God always before us like a rule, and believe nothing but that which it teacheth, love nothing but that which it prescribeth, hate nothing but that which it forbiddeth, do nothing but that which it commandeth." If you read the Puritans regularly, their focus on the Scriptures will become contagious, teaching you how to yield wholehearted allegiance to the Bible's message.

2. The Puritans integrated biblical doctrine into daily life. The Puritans did this in three ways. First, they addressed the mind. They believed that an anti-intellectual gospel quickly becomes an empty, formless gospel that doesn't move beyond "felt needs." Second, they confronted the conscience. The Puritans were masters at naming specific sins, then asking questions to press home conviction of those sins in order to drive men to Christ. Third, they engaged the heart. They preached and wrote with affectionate warmth, seeking to move the hearts of their hearers with the truths of God's Word.

3. The Puritans loved Christ and exalted in His beauty. Samuel Rutherford wrote: "Put the beauty of ten thousand worlds of paradises, like the Garden of Eden in one; put all trees, all flowers, all smells, all colors, all tastes, all joys, all loveliness, all sweetness in one. O what a fair and excellent thing would that be? And yet it would be less to that fair and dearest well-beloved Christ than one drop of rain to the whole seas, rivers, lakes, and foundations of ten thousand earths." If you would know Christ better and love Him more fully, immerse yourself in Puritan literature.

4. The Puritans knew how to handle trials. We learn from the Puritans that we need affliction to humble us, to teach us what sin is, and to bring us to God. As Robert Leighton wrote, "Affliction is the diamond dust that heaven polishes its jewels with." The Puritans teach us how God's rod of affliction is His means to write Christ's image more fully upon us, so that we may be partakers of His holiness.

5. The Puritans lived in two worlds. They lived with eternity in sight. The Puritans believed that we should have heaven "in our eye" throughout our earthly pilgrimage, taking seriously the dual reality (now/not-yet) of the New Testament. By reading them, we learn that the joy of heaven makes amends for any losses and crosses that we must endure on earth if we follow Christ. Their writings inspire a forward-looking hope.

How to Use This Workbook

This workbook has been designed to supplement the 35 video lessons on Puritanism. We have intentionally designed it to be useful in a number of different contexts, including personal devotions, homeschooling, study groups, and Sunday School.

Each chapter focuses on a particular lesson and is divided into five sections:

1. Meditate – Here you will find a Puritan quotation along with a pertinent passage of Scripture for meditation. Take a few minutes to prayerfully ponder the passage in this section and record any thoughts or applications that come to mind.

2. Learn – This section contains material on the subject covered in the video lesson. Some of this will be review from the lesson, but will also contain supplementary material to further whet your appetite for these rich themes.

3. Reflect – We have provided questions here for personal reflection and examination. This section is intended to help you digest the lesson material and apply it to your soul and life. We are after what the Puritans called "experiential religion."

4. Discuss – Next are questions for group discussion, though they can also be used for personal study. This section aims to be less soul searching and more theological and practical, helping you think through the lesson material in its application to the church today.

5. Read – In this final section you will find a brief bibliography with some of the most helpful primary and secondary sources to pursue for further study. The goal of these lessons is not to be ends in themselves, but means to get you to read the Puritans for yourself, if you are not doing so already.

It is our hope and prayer that these lessons will be used to ignite within you a passion for the triune God whom the Puritans delighted in proclaiming.

—Joel Beeke and Nicholas Thompson

PART ONE

Puritan Pastors and Influential Figures

William Perkins

Lesson Given by Stephen Yuille

Meditate

"Our first and principle joy," wrote William Perkins, "must be that we are in God's favor, reconciled to God by Christ.... And all other petty joys must flow from this, and be suitable to it." Christians, concluded Perkins, are to "be ravished with joy in Christ." Meditate on Philippians 4:4.

Learn

Perkins has often been called the Father of Puritanism. Historian William Haller wrote of Perkins's *Works*, "No books, it is fair to say, were more often to be found upon the shelves of succeeding generations of preachers, and the name of no preacher recurs more often in later Puritan literature."

His Life

1558 Perkins is born in the village of Marston Jabbett, Warwickshire.

1577 He begins studies at Christ's College, where he is converted to Christ.

1581 Perkins graduates with his bachelor's degree from Cambridge.

1584 Upon graduating with his master's degree, Perkins is ordained to the ministry and made a fellow at Christ's College.

1585 He is appointed lecturer of Great St. Andrew's Church.

1590 Perkins is called to serve as Dean of Christ's College.

1595 He resigns his fellowship at Christ's College in order to marry Timothye Cradock, but continues to preach at Great St. Andrews Church until his death.

1602 Perkins dies of kidney stone complications at the age of forty-four.

1608 His *Works* are first published in a 3-volume set.

Did You Know?

- Like Chaderton, his mentor, Perkins worked to purify the established church from within rather than joining Puritans who advocated separation. He would remain in the Church of England to the end of his life.

- Perkins was not only a powerful preacher and gifted theologian, but he also possessed a keen ability to counsel people with the Scriptures, offering pastoral wisdom in their spiritual struggles.

- It is said that on the first page of each of his sermon manuscripts he would write himself the message: "Thou art a Minister of the Word: Mind thy business."

- After his death, Perkins's writings were translated into Dutch, Latin, German, Spanish, French, Italian, Gaelic, Welsh, Hungarian, and Czech. This led one to declare that "his books spoke more tongues than the author ever knew."

His Legacy

J. I. Packer writes, "No Puritan author save Richard Baxter ever sold better than Perkins, and no Puritan thinker ever did more to share and solidify historic Puritanism itself." Below we will look at three ways Perkins left his indelible mark upon the church.

Proclaimer of Grace

Stephen Yuille argues that Perkins was instrumental in securing and advancing reformation in the Church of England. One of the primary areas in which he furthered the cause of biblical truth was in his exposition of God's grace in salvation. Both Rome and the 39 Articles had left room for man's meritorious works in either election or justification, seeing redemption as a mixture of the divine and the human. But Perkins believed that from beginning to end man's salvation comes from God alone. Thus, he branded Roman Catholicism "an enemy of the grace of God because it exalts the liberty of man's will, and extenuates the grace of God, and joins the merit of works as a concurring cause with the grace of God in the procurement of eternal life." He also denied article 17 of the 39 Articles because it "placed the cause of God's predestination in man." In this way, Perkins was instrumental in the preservation and promotion of the biblical gospel.

Promoter of Piety

While exalting in the exhaustive sovereignty of God's grace in man's salvation, Perkins never tired of stressing man's responsibility and the necessity of Christian piety. He wrote, "Saving knowledge in religion is experimental, and he that is truly founded upon Christ feels the power and efficacy of His death and resurrection, effectually causing the death of sin, and the life of grace which both appear by new obedience." For Perkins, theology was not a purely academic discipline, but was absolutely crucial to the development of godliness in Christ. Through his emphasis on holiness, H. C. Porter writes, Perkins "moulded the piety of a whole nation."

Paradigm for Ministry

Perkins believed that the woeful state of the church in his day was explained in large measure by the lack of capable pastors. This led him to make the training of young men for ministry a chief priority. Through his labors at Cambridge, he influenced a generation of young men, including Richard Sibbes, John Cotton, John Preston, and William Ames. In fact, Cotton considered Perkins's ministry the "one good reason why there came so many excellent preachers out of Cambridge in England, more than out of Oxford." He devised a very simple structure in preaching and writing: exposition, doctrines, and uses. Rather than using words that may impress the listener but leave their minds uncomprehending, Perkins said that with regard to preaching, "the plainer, the better." Through his instruction and example, a generation of faithful, plain, and powerful preachers were raised up.

Reflect

1. Perkins devoted his pulpit and pen to extolling and defending the grace of God in salvation. Have you been overtaken by the free grace of God in the gospel? What is the proper response to the realization that you contribute nothing to your salvation, save your own sin?

2. Yuille speaks of Perkins's concern over the Church of England, which affirmed the doctrines of Christianity intellectually, but had so little vitality. Does your faith in Christ work by love (Gal. 5:6), thereby fulfilling the law (Rom. 13:8)? Is there evidence of God's life-giving, sanctifying grace in your life?

3. Perkins famously exhorted his fellow ministers to "preach one Christ by Christ to the praise of Christ." Are you satisfied with anything less than this from the pulpit? Do you hunger after Christ-empowered and Christ-exalting preaching?

Discuss

1. Perkins taught that fallen man's will apart from regenerating grace is a "bound free-will." In other words, we are free because our choices are our own, but our choices are not free from our darkened mind and hardened heart. How does such a view influence our approach to preaching to, evangelizing, and praying for the unconverted?

2. Article 17 of the 39 Articles taught that God elects those whom He foresees will believe in Christ. How does this distort the biblical doctrine of predestination? What Scripture texts would you use to argue against it?

3. Perkins defined theology as "the science of living blessedly forever." What did he mean by this? How does such a definition promote godliness among God's people?

4. In Perkins's mind, equipping men for the ministry was of utmost importance for the church. What is the role of the local church in the training of men for the gospel ministry?

Read

Primary Sources

Perkins, William. *The Works of William Perkins*. 10 volumes. Edited by Joel Beeke and Derek Thomas. Grand Rapids: Reformation Heritage Books, 2014–.

Perkins, William. *The Art of Prophesying*. Edinburgh: Banner of Truth Trust, 1996.

Secondary Sources

Beeke, Joel and Stephen Yuille. *William Perkins*. Darlington, England: Evangelical Press, 2015.

Patterson, W. B. *William Perkins and the Making of a Protestant England*. Oxford: Oxford University Press, 2014.

Yuille, Stephen. *Living Blessedly Forever: The Sermon on the Mount and the Puritan Piety of William Perkins*. Grand Rapids: Reformation Heritage Books, 2012.

Richard Sibbes

Lesson Given by Mark Dever

Meditate

Sibbes exhorted his people, "Measure not God's love and favor by your own feeling. The sun shines as clearly in the darkest day as it does in the brightest. The difference is not in the sun, but in some clouds which hinder the manifestation of the light thereof." Meditate on Ephesians 2:4–5.

Learn

Sibbes was known by many as "the heavenly Doctor," due to his godly preaching and heavenly manner of life. A contemporary said of him, "Heaven was in him, before he was in heaven." Maurice Roberts describes Sibbes's theology as "the fuel of some great combustion engine, always passing into flame and so being converted into energy thereby to serve God and, even more, to enjoy and relish God with the soul."

His Life

1577	Richard Sibbes is born at Tostock, Suffolk.
1602	He earns a master's degree at Cambridge, having already obtained a bachelor's three years earlier.
1603	Sibbes is converted through the preaching of Paul Baynes, the successor of William Perkins at the Church of St. Andrews.
1608	He is ordained as a deacon and a priest in the Church of England.
1609	Being elected as a college preacher, Sibbes begins to rise in prominence as a preacher and lecturer.
1610	Sibbes takes up the position of lecturer at Holy Trinity Church in Cambridge.
1617	He receives a call to London to be a lecturer for Gray's Inn.
1626	While continuing his preaching at Gray's Inn, Sibbes also becomes the master of St. Catharine's College in Cambridge.
1633	He becomes the vicar of Holy Trinity in Cambridge at the invitation of King Charles I.
1635	Sibbes dies from an illness on July 5.

Did You Know?

- Sibbes's father, though a Christian, was frustrated by Richard's interest in books as a young child and wanted him to follow in his steps as a repairer of wooden wheels.

- During his years at Holy Trinity, Sibbes helped turn Thomas Goodwin away from Arminianism and was instrumental in John Preston's shift from "witty preaching" to plain, spiritual preaching.

- Sibbes never married, but he established an astonishing network of friendships that included godly ministers, noted lawyers, and parliamentary leaders.

- He began his will and testament the day before his death with the words, "I commend and bequeath my soul into the hands of my gracious Savior, who hath redeemed it with his most precious blood, and appears now in heaven to receive it."

His Legacy

Dever refers to Sibbes as a "sweet expounder" of God's grace and love in Christ. He never seemed to tire of impressing upon his hearers the grand truth of God's merciful affection toward hell-worthy sinners.

Gospel: The Display of God's Love in Christ

For Sibbes, the chief manifestation of God's love was the gospel. He states, "You see how full of love he was. What drew him from heaven to earth, and so to his cross and to his grave, but love to mankind?" Sibbes was amazed that God would love sinners to such an extent that He would send His Son to take on flesh and suffer in their stead. He had drunken deeply of the sweetness of this grace and it thus permeated all of his preaching. The gospel, in Sibbes's mind, was first and foremost a declaration of divine love.

Regeneration: The Perceiving of God's Love in Christ

Sibbes upheld that "a carnal eye will never see spiritual things." When sinners, however, are graciously quickened by the Spirit of God, they are overtaken with "the sight of their misery and the sight of God's love in Christ." The divine love and grace which could not be perceived before become experientially known via regeneration. Sibbes believed that this ordinarily happens through the preaching of the gospel: "As the minister speaks to the ear, Christ speaks, opens, and unlocks the heart at the same time; and gives it power to open, not from itself, but from Christ." Christ, by His Spirit, transforms the souls of sinful men to see and receive the love of God in the gospel.

Sanctification: The Response to God's Love in Christ

But how do you know if you have truly received the love of God? Sibbes would say that one great evidence of God's love for you is a corresponding love to God. He reasons, "When we look upon the mercy of God in Christ, it kindleth love, and love kindleth love, as fire kindleth fire." God's love in the soul is like a fire that ignites love toward God. And this apprehension of and affectionate response to the love of God is foundational to a life of holiness. Sibbes writes, "Whatsoever we do else, if it be not stirred by the Spirit, apprehending the love of God in Christ, it is but morality. What are all our performances if they be not out of love to God?" If our works are not flowing from the love of God, then they are not pleasing to God.

Reflect

1. Sibbes once wrote, "With the same love that God loves Christ, he loves all his." Do you ever question God's love for you? If so, why? How does the gospel dispel your doubts?

2. Dever spoke of Sibbes's exposition of God's mercy in *The Bruised Reed*, encouraging those with small faith to not look to the proportion of their faith but to the gracious Christ who is the object of faith. Where do your eyes turn when you sense the weakness of your faith?

3. Does God's love in Christ stir within you a desire to please Him and live for His glory? Is such divine love a primary motivation for your service of Him and His Church?

1. How does Sibbes's understanding of the love of God in the gospel and the Spirit's work in regeneration inform our evangelism?

2. Sibbes argues that if our works be not flowing from an apprehension of God's love, then they will be mere "morality." What does he mean by this? How does grasping the love of God fuel our sanctification?

3. If our good works are to be done as a loving response to God's love, what are we to do when we don't sense God's love and find our own hearts cold and loveless?

4. Sibbes was known as a gracious and humble man who avoided the controversies of his day as much as possible. What can we learn from him here? How might his experience of God's grace and love have worked in him such humility?

_____

Primary Sources

Sibbes, Richard. *The Bruised Reed.* Edinburgh: Banner of Truth Trust, 1998.

Sibbes, Richard. *Glorious Freedom.* Edinburgh: Banner of Truth Trust, 2000.

Sibbes, Richard. *The Works of Richard Sibbes.* 7 volumes. Edinburgh: Banner of Truth Trust, 2001.

Secondary Sources

Dever, Mark. *The Affectionate Theology of Richard Sibbes.* Sanford, FL: Reformation Trust, 2018.

Beeke, Joel and Mark Jones. "Richard Sibbes on Entertaining the Holy Spirit." In *A Puritan Theology: Doctrine for Life,* 573–86. Grand Rapids: Reformation Heritage Books, 2012.

Oliver Cromwell

Lesson Given by Michael Haykin

Meditate

Recounting the Lord's gracious dealings with him, Cromwell wrote, "One beam in a dark place hath exceeding much refreshment in it:—blessed be his name for shining upon so dark a heart as mine! You know what my manner of life hath been. Oh, I lived in and loved darkness, and hated the light. I was a chief, the chief of sinners. This is true; I hated godliness, yet God had mercy on me. O the riches of his mercy!" Meditate on 1 Timothy 1:15–17.

Learn

D. Martyn Lloyd-Jones once said, "That great period during Cromwell's Protectorate... was one of the most amazing epochs in the whole history of [England]. To me it was certainly one of the most glorious.... Oliver Cromwell is a man whom we do not honor as we should."

His Life

1599   Cromwell is born at Huntingdon to Robert and Elizabeth Cromwell.

1620   He marries Elizabeth Bourchier in London.

1628   Cromwell is elected a member of parliament for Huntingdon.

1629   Somewhere around this time he is converted to Christ.

1640   Cromwell becomes a member of parliament for Cambridge.

1642   After the civil war breaks out, Cromwell forms a troop of cavalry.

1644   He is promoted as lieutenant-general of the cavalry in the Eastern Association army.

1653   He becomes Lord Protector (i.e., head of state) of the Commonwealth of England.

1657   Cromwell is offered kingship but he turns it down.

1658   He dies on September 3 due to health complications.

Did You Know?

- Richard Baxter said of Cromwell's army, "He had a special care to get religious men into his troop: These men...did prove so valiant, that as far as I could learn, they never once ran away before an enemy."

- Though a strong military and political leader, Cromwell possessed a passionate love for Christ. He wrote to his newly married daughter, "Dear Heart, press on; let not husband, let not anything cool thy affections after Christ. I hope he will be an occasion to inflame them. That which is best worthy of love in thy husband is that of the image of Christ he bears. Look on that, and love it best, and all the rest for that."

- On his deathbed, Cromwell said, "I would be willing to live to be farther serviceable to God and his people; but my work is done. Yet God will be with his people."

- Though buried in Westminster Abby in 1658, his body was dug up by Royalists, hung on a gallows, and cast in an unmarked grave in 1661.

His Legacy

His Sense of Unworthiness

One cannot read Cromwell's letters and addresses without being impressed with the low view that he possessed of himself. He never seemed to get over the fact that God would take a sinful creature like himself and call him into Christ's service. Writing to John Cotton, he said, "I am a poor weak creature, and not worthy the name of a worm.... Indeed, my dear friend, between you and me, you know not me, my weakness, my inordinate passions, my unskillfulness and everyway unfitness to my work. Yet, yet the Lord, who will have mercy on whom he will, does as you see!" He bore this sense of unworthiness to the end, confessing on his deathbed, "I think I am the poorest wretch that lives."

His Faith in Providence

According to Cromwell, everything that happens in human history is from the Lord. Writing concerning the combat in Ireland, he said, "Truly our work is neither from our brains nor from our courage and strength, but we follow the Lord who goeth before, and gather what he scattereth, that so all may appear to be from him." Winning the Battle of Marston Moor in 1644, he claimed the victory to be "a great favor from the Lord." When the English, however, were defeated by the Spanish on the island of Hispaniola in 1655, Cromwell concluded that the defeat was God's punishment upon England for their sin. While Cromwell rightly teaches us to acknowledge God's providential government in all things, he ought to have taken much greater care in interpreting providence.

His Propagation of Piety

Cromwell was a man of godliness and he everywhere sought to propagate the same. It is common in his letters to his wife and children to find exhortations such as this, written to his son in 1650: "Seek the Lord and his face continually: let this be the business of your life and strength, and let all things be subservient...to this." In a speech before the members of parliament, he said, "It ought to be the longing of our hearts to see men brought to own the interest of Jesus Christ. And give me leave to say that, if I know anything in the world, what is there more like to win the people to the interest of Jesus Christ, to the love of godliness, but an humble and godly conversation?" In his family and among his troops, Cromwell was always seeking to lead people to Christ that they might live for Christ.

His Promotion of Religious Toleration

Cromwell fought for religious liberty in his day. Before Parliament, he said, "Is not Liberty of Conscience in religion a fundamental? Every sect saith, 'Oh! Give me liberty.' But give him it, and to his power he will not yield it to anybody else. Where is our ingenuity? Truly, that's a thing ought to be very reciprocal." No man should be forced to violate his conscience in religious matters so long as he remains an upright citizen. Cromwell even stated that "he had rather that Mahometanism were permitted amongst us than that one of God's children should be persecuted."

Reflect

1. Do you struggle with high-mindedness and pride? How could a fuller experience of God's grace deepen your sense of lowliness and unworthiness?

2. Is your soul governed by a quiet trust in God's sovereign rule over all things? Are you quick to submit to His all-wise providence in your life? Or do you often question and grumble against it?

3. Cromwell sought to propagate piety, not only in the church but in his home and among his troops. Are you actively pursuing the same among your family members and coworkers? What are some specific ways you could be more intentional in this?

Discuss

1. Cromwell was quick to refer to himself as a "poor worm and a weak servant" while also glorying in his salvation in Christ. Can a Christian's sense of sinfulness and unworthiness become extreme and unhealthy? What are the marks of a healthy identity in Christ?

2. What can we learn from Cromwell's providentialism? How are Christians to interpret the working out of God's will in history?

3. Cromwell argued that a foundation stone of religion is liberty of conscience. Why must the conscience not be coerced in religious matters? Is religious toleration, as propagated by Cromwell, a biblical concept?

4. Michael Haykin states that Cromwell was a quintessential Puritan, except in his ecclesiology, since he never belonged to a church. Is it possible for one to be a healthy Christian without being attached to a local congregation?

Read

Haykin, Michael, ed. *"To honor God": The Spirituality of Oliver Cromwell.* Dundas, Ontario: Joshua Press, 1999.

Roots, Ivan, ed. *Speeches of Oliver Cromwell.* London: J.M. Dent & Sons Ltd., 1989.

Fraser, Antonia. *Cromwell: The Lord Protector.* New York: Alfred A. Knopf, 1974.

Hill, Christopher. *God's Englishman: Oliver Cromwell and the English Revolution.* New York: Harper & Row, 1972.

Paul, Robert. *The Lord Protector: Religion and Politics in the Life of Oliver Cromwell.* Grand Rapids: Eerdmans, 1955.

Thomas Goodwin

Lesson Given by Joel Beeke

Meditate

According to Goodwin, the Bible "doth, as it were, take our hands, and lay them upon Christ's breast, and let us feel how his heart beats and his bowels yearn towards us, even now he is in glory–the very scope of these words being manifestly to encourage believers against all that may discourage them, from the consideration of Christ's heart towards them now in heaven." Meditate on Hebrews 4:15.

Learn

"In Goodwin," states Michael Reeves, "a simply awesome theological intellect was wielded by the tender heart of a pastor." Alexander Whyte commended him as "the greatest pulpit exegete of Paul that has ever lived."

His Life

1600   Goodwin is born in Rollesby to God-fearing parents.

1620   He is converted by means of a funeral sermon preached on Luke 19:41–42.

1628   Goodwin is appointed lecturer at Trinity Church, succeeding Sibbes and eventually becoming the minister there.

1634   Being forced to resign due to political pressures, he moves to London and continues to preach there.

1639   Goodwin, on account of increasing restrictions against preaching, moves to the Netherlands and begins to minister to English refugees.

1641   He returns to England and begins to pastor a church in London.

1643   He is appointed as a member of the Westminster Assembly, proving to be very influential in its proceedings.

1650   Goodwin becomes president of Magdalen College, Oxford.

1658   With Oliver Cromwell's permission, Goodwin helps draw up the Savoy Declaration of Faith and Order.

1660   He leaves Oxford and starts another Independent congregation in London.

1679   Goodwin dies in London, having lived amid some of the most remarkable events in England's ecclesiastical and political history.

Did You Know?

- Richard Sibbes, who was greatly influential in Goodwin's life, once told him, "Young man, if ever you would do good, you must preach the gospel and the free grace of God in Christ Jesus." Goodwin took this exhortation to heart and ordered the whole of his ministry around it.

- Records of the Westminster Assembly indicate that Goodwin gave more addresses than any other divine—357 in all.

- The sorrow produced from losing the majority of his personal library in the fire of London resulted in his writing a work entitled, *Patience and Its Perfect Work under Sudden and Sore Trials.*

- Some of Goodwin's final words were, "I could not have imagined I should have had such a measure of faith in this hour; no, I could never have imagined it. My bow abides in strength."

His Legacy

Goodwin is reputedly one of the most Christological of all the Puritans. Christ was always in his mind's eye and upon his tongue and pen. But nowhere does he so set forth the beauties of Christ as in his most popular work, *The Heart of Christ in Heaven towards Sinners on Earth.*

Christ's Gracious Proof

Goodwin believed that the Scriptures "open a window into Christ's heart." Though Christ has been exalted in the heavens, He has not forgotten His people. Christ's heart remains full of mercy even while at His Father's right hand. In fact, Goodwin argued from John 13–17 that the purpose for which Christ ascended to heaven was to secure our happiness as believers and to prepare a place for us. Not only that, but Christ committed to His bride the care of His "dearest friend," the Comforter. All the works of the Holy Spirit testify of Christ's present love for His church. And he ever lives at the Father's right hand to intercede on her behalf. The revelation of the glorified Christ's care for His people is amazingly comprehensive and comforting.

Christ's Expanded Affections

Always a careful theologian, Goodwin made clear that Christ is not still suffering in heaven. His humiliation was completed at the cross and tomb. In His exaltation, His human nature is glorified and free from all pain. Yet he remains a person with human emotions and a human body. And having entered into glory, Goodwin remarks, "his human affections of love and pity are enlarged in solidity, strength, and reality." So Christ is not hurt by our sufferings and sins, but His human soul responds to them with glorious, beautiful tenderness. He is "able and powerful to take our miseries into his heart, though glorified, and so to be affected with them, as if he suffered with us."

Christ's Longing to Return

Goodwin wrote, "[Christ] took our flesh and carried it into heaven, and left us his Spirit on earth, both being pawns and earnests that we should follow." Christ's heart in heaven longs for that great day when He will come again to take His people to be with Him forever. "He will not stay a minute longer than he must," argues Goodwin. "He tarries only till he has throughout the ages by his intercession prepared every room for each saint, that he may entertain them all at once together and have them all about him." Christ's affection for His people moves Him with intense longing to bring them to their eternal abode.

Reflect

1. Goodwin defined the Christian life as "a habitual sight of [Christ]." Are you captivated by the beauty and glory of Jesus? What steps could you take to see Him more clearly and adore Him more heartily?

2. In what ways do the expanded affections of the exalted Christ comfort and encourage you in your earthly pilgrimage?

3. Not only does Christ long to come back for His bride, but His bride longs and looks for His coming (Titus 2:13). How often do you think about Christ's second coming? Are you eagerly awaiting and anticipating His return?

Discuss

1. Christ-centered piety is a major theme in Goodwin's writing. What is the relationship between Christ and piety (i.e., godliness)? How does one pursue sanctification in a Christ-centered way?

2. Because of His love toward her, Christ desires to come for His bride. Yet it is the same love which causes Him to delay His coming. How do both this strong yearning and this patient delaying evidence Christ's heart of compassion? What is the gracious purpose behind Christ prolonging the time before His second coming?

3. Goodwin said, "Your very sins move [Christ] to pity more than to anger." How does the gracious heart of Christ and His being grieved by our sin produce a strong incentive not to sin?

4. Why is Christ's heavenly ministry and heart toward His people so little preached on today? What affect has this had upon the church?

Read

Primary Sources

Goodwin, Thomas. *Christ Set Forth and the Heart of Christ in Heaven towards Sinners on Earth*. Fearn, UK: Christian Focus, 2011.

Goodwin, Thomas. *The Works of Thomas Goodwin*. 12 volumes. Grand Rapids: Reformation Heritage Books, 2006.

Secondary Sources

Beeke, Joel and Mark Jones, eds. *A Habitual Sight of Him: The Christ-Centered Piety of Thomas Goodwin*. Grand Rapids: Reformation Heritage Books, 2009.

Beeke, Joel and Mark Jones. "Thomas Goodwin on Christ's Beautiful Heart." In *A Puritan Theology: Doctrine for Life*, 387–400. Grand Rapids: Reformation Heritage Books, 2012.

Jones, Mark. *Why Heaven Kissed Earth: The Christology of Thomas Goodwin*. Gottingen: Vandenhoeck & Ruprecht, 2010.

Richard Baxter

Lesson Given by Joel Beeke and J. I. Packer

Meditate

Nearing death, Baxter wrote, "My Lord, I have nothing to do in this world, but to seek and serve thee; I have nothing to do with a heart and its affections but to breathe after thee; I have nothing to do with my tongue and pen, but to speak to thee, and for thee, and to publish thy glory and thy will." Meditate on Colossians 3:17.

Learn

J. I. Packer once referred to Baxter as "the most outstanding pastor, evangelist, and writer on practical and devotional themes that Puritanism produced."

His Life

1615   Baxter is born in Rowton, Shropshire, to Richard Baxter Sr. and Beatrice Adeney.

1638   After an informal education, he is ordained in the Church of England.

1639   Baxter becomes an assistant minister at Bridgnorth, Shoropshire.

1641   He is called to be the lecturer at Kidderminster as a result of the corruption of the present minister there.

1642   Due to hostility within the congregation and the dangers of civil war, Baxter leaves Kidderminster.

1645   He becomes a chaplain of the Parliamentary army.

1647   Overtaken by a life-threatening illness, Baxter leaves the army, returning to Kidderminster where he would labor for 13 more years.

1660   Baxter leaves Kidderminster. He would never again gather a congregation of his own, but continues preaching, lecturing, and writing until his dying day.

1662   Upon the heels of his ejection from the Church of England by the Act of Uniformity, Baxter marries Margaret Charlton, one of his converts.

1669   Baxter is imprisoned. Though released relatively quickly, he would be imprisoned multiple times and suffer continual persecution for his nonconformist preaching and writing.

1681   Baxter's wife passes away, causing him immense grief.

1691   Baxter, suffering great sickness and pain, dies on December 8.

Did You Know?

- Richard Sibbes's *The Bruised Reed* was instrumental in Baxter's teenage years. He writes, "Sibbes opened more the love of God to me, and gave me a livelier apprehension of the mystery of redemption and how much I was beholden to Jesus Christ."

- In his early years, Baxter struggled with assurance of salvation because he did not know the day or hour he had been converted. But he eventually concluded rightly: "God breaketh not all men's hearts alike."

- Baxter suffered from immense physical ailments throughout his ministry, including tuberculosis, migraines, digestive disorders, and kidney stones. He said that he had "seldom an hour free from pain" for the last fifty-five years of his life.

- Baxter's *Call to the Unconverted* sold 20,000 copies within the first year it was published and was the means by which many where brought to faith in Christ during his life.

His Legacy

Serious Preaching

When Baxter first came to Kidderminster, he said that "they had hardly ever had any lively serious preaching among them." Through his faithful proclamation of God's Word the town was turned on its head. Baxter was passionate about preaching because he believed it was the primary means that God uses to save sinners and sanctify saints. Preaching, therefore, was a very solemn task for him. He once said, "I preached as never sure to preach again, and as a dying man to dying men." He considered every sermon to be the last he would preach and the last his people would hear. And this caused him to implore his hearers to come to Christ with all the affection and persuasive powers his redeemed soul possessed. In fact, Spurgeon wrote, "If you want to know the art of pleading, read Baxter."

Catechetical Teaching

While Baxter believed in the primacy of preaching, he knew that his hearers often needed to have God's truth personally impressed upon their souls to meet particular circumstances. He wrote, "Some ignorant persons, who have been so long unprofitable hearers, have got more knowledge and remorse of conscience in half an hour's close disclosure, than they did from ten year's public preaching." Baxter and his assistants spent two days a week visiting with parishioners and catechizing them. He said of these visits, "Few families went from me without some tears, or seemingly serious promises [to strive] for a godly life."

Zealous Ministry

Baxter's view of the ministry was put to paper in his famous *The Reformed Pastor*. He begins by impressing upon his readers the need for converted pastors: "It is the common danger and calamity of the Church...to have so many men become preachers before they are Christians...to preach an unknown Christ, to pray through an unknown Spirit." He then with penetrating conviction calls his fellow ministers to keep a careful watch over themselves and their flocks. Spurgeon, struggling with his own lack of zeal in the ministry, once enjoined his wife, "Go to the study and fetch down Baxter's *Reformed Pastor*, and read some of it to me. Perhaps that will quicken my sluggish heart."

Reflect

1. Due to a life-threatening illness, Baxter found himself bed-ridden with eternity upon his doorstep. It was here that he wrote one of his most well-known works, *The Saints' Everlasting Rest*. How has the Lord used hard providences to accomplish His purposes in your life? What is a time when God worked a peculiarly difficult trial for good?

2. Baxter considered preaching to be a profoundly serious matter. What does it look like to listen to preaching as a dying man? How would it affect the way you hear and receive God's Word if you knew it was the last sermon you would ever hear?

3. Joel Beeke mentions Baxter's response to the praise for his books while on his deathbed: "I was a pen in God's hand; what praise is due to a pen?" Have you reckoned with the fact that all your gifts and graces come from God? How can you use the abilities God has given you to point away from yourself to Him?

_____

_____

_____

_____

_____

_____

_____

Discuss

1. Baxter's father, initially a negative influence upon him, became instrumental in his conversion to Christ. What lessons and encouragements can be drawn from this for parents today?

2. For Baxter, preaching entailed earnest pleading. Is this taught in the Scriptures? Should such importunate entreating be practiced by preachers today? What are its strengths and dangers?

3. Baxter warned ministers of the "sly and subtle insinuating enemy" called pride. How are ministers particularly susceptible to pride? What are some God-given remedies for pride, whether in a minister or a layperson?

4. Referring to Baxter's flawed theology (particularly in the area of justification), Edward Donnelly writes, "Baxter is no more of a perfect exemplar than any other son of Adam." What can we learn from Baxter's imperfection?

Read

Primary Sources

Baxter, Richard. *The Reformed Pastor.* Edinburgh: Banner of Truth Trust, 1999.

Baxter, Richard. *The Saints' Everlasting Rest.* Fearn, UK: Christian Focus, 1999.

Baxter, Richard. *The Autobiography of Richard Baxter.* London: J. M. Dent, 1925.

Baxter, Richard. *The Practical Works of Richard Baxter.* 4 volumes. Ligonier, PA: Soli Deo Gloria, 1990.

Secondary Sources

Packer, J. I. *A Grief Sanctified: Through Sorrow to Eternal Hope, Including Richard Baxter's Timeless Memoir of His Wife's Life and Death.* Wheaton, IL: Crossway Books, 2002.

Powicke, Frederick J. *A Life of the Reverend Richard Baxter 1615–1691.* Boston: Houghton Mifflin Co., 1924.

Salisbury, Vance. *Good Mister Baxter: Sketches of Effective, Gospel-Centered Leadership from the Life of Richard Baxter.* Nevada City, CA: Piety Hill Press, 2007.

John Owen

Lesson Given by Sinclair Ferguson

Meditate

Owen exhorts, "Set faith at work on Christ for the killing of thy sin." Meditate on Romans 8:13.

Learn

Sinclair Ferguson refers to Owen as "one of the greatest spiritual masters, probably the greatest of the Puritan thinkers, and a man whose writings continue to be enormously relevant to the twenty-first century." He was, as Spurgeon called him, "the Prince of the Puritans."

His Life

1616   John Owen is born in Stadham, near Oxford.

1628   He enters Queen's College, Oxford, at the age of twelve.

1637   Owen leaves Oxford, becoming a private tutor and chaplain.

1642   He is brought to assurance of faith through an unknown preacher in London.

1643   Owen begins his writing career (publishing his first book) and takes up a call to pastor in Fordham, where he would wed Mary Rooke.

1646   He becomes vicar of St. Peter's, Coggeshall, and preaches before Parliament.

1649   Owen accompanies Oliver Cromwell to Ireland as his chaplain.

1650   He is appointed as an official preacher to the state.

1651   Owen begins working at Oxford University, eventually becoming the vice chancellor.

1660   He leaves Oxford University, retiring in Stadham where he continued to preach.

1665   Owen pastors a small congregation in London, preaching and writing there until his death.

1683   John Owen dies just as his work on the glory of Christ goes to press.

Did You Know?

- During his university studies, Owen maintained such a rigorous schedule that he only slept an average of four hours a night. He would later regret this for the damage it caused to his health.

- Only one of Owen's eleven children lived to adulthood. He knew intimately the immense grief produced by losing children.

- While teaching at Oxford, Owen refused to wear the traditional cap and hood worn by professors. He thought it smelled of Roman Catholicism and thus dressed no different than his students.

- The inscription of Owen's grave stone refers to him as "a traveler on earth who grasped God like one in heaven." What a statement!

His Legacy

John Owen, according to Ferguson, was a man controlled by the "basic principle that at the heart of living the Christian life and worshiping God is the knowledge of God according to Scripture." In his preaching, teaching, and writing, Owen displayed a profound devotion to the Word of God. His strong intellect wedded to a Spirit-worked faith in the Bible resulted in thousands of pages of spiritual riches which continue to bear fruit in the lives of God's people today. Ferguson highlights three areas of Owen's thought particularly worthy of consideration:

Christ's Glorious Person

Expounding John 17:24, Owen writes, "The beholding of the glory of Christ is one of the greatest privileges and advancements that believers are capable of in this world, or that which is to come.... For here in this life, beholding his glory, they are changed or transformed into the likeness of it (2 Cor. 3:18); and hereafter they shall be for ever 'like him,' because they 'shall see him as he is' (1 John 3:1–2)." For Owen, the Christian life was one of beholding, delighting in, and becoming like the Savior.

Thus, the believer ought to meditate regularly on the person of Jesus as He is revealed in the pages of Scripture. "Upon this," he said, "do our present comforts and future blessedness depend."

Communion with God

Owen was convinced that the doctrine of the Trinity was no abstract, scholastic truth, but that it rather pervaded the very essence of the Christian life. Through Christ's mediatorial work, the believer partakes in distinct communion with each person of the triune Deity. Owen defined such communion as God's "communication of himself unto us, with our returnal unto him of that which he requireth and acccepteth, flowing from that union which in Jesus Christ we have with him." It consisted of a relationship of mutual exchange between the believer and God. From 2 Corinthians 13:14, Owen concluded that the Christian enjoys communion with the Father in love, with the Son in grace, and with the Holy Spirit in comfort.

Mortification of Sin

Because of the presence of remaining corruption in the hearts of believers, they must be ever active in putting sin to death. Owen remarks, "If sin be subtle, watchful, strong, and always at work in the business of killing our souls, and we be slothful, negligent, foolish, in proceeding to the ruin thereof, can we expect a comfortable event? There is not a day but sin foils or is foiled, prevails or is prevailed on; and it will be so whilst we live in this world." Either we put sin to death, or sin will destroy us.

Reflect

1. Ferguson describes Owen as one who "ransacked Scripture." Are you a diligent student of God's Word? How could you grow in this area?

2. What comes into your mind when you think about Christ? Owen said that His glory is "the principle object of our faith, love, delight, and admiration." Can that be said of you?

3. One of Owen's most oft-quoted statements is, "Be killing sin or sin will be killing you." Are you daily striving by God's grace to put sin to death? Are there areas where sin seems to be getting the upper hand? What are you doing about it?

Discuss

_____

1. What lessons can we learn from the unknown, nameless man who preached the sermon under which Owen was brought to assurance of faith?

2. Owen taught that the Christian's present comfort depends upon a spiritual sight of Christ's glory in the Scriptures. How does knowing and beholding the beauty of Christ's person comfort and strengthen the souls of God's people, particularly in times of affliction?

3. According to Owen, why is the doctrine of the Trinity an eminently practical doctrine? How ought the triunity of God orient our lives as individuals and as the church?

4. Owen speaks of communion with God as a "mutual communication in giving and receiving" between God and the Christian. What does this mean? What are the implications for understanding your relationship with God to be one of mutual exchange?

Read

Primary Sources

Owen, John. *Meditations and Discourses on the Glory of Christ. In The Works of John Owen,* 1:273–461. Edited by William H. Goold. Edinburgh: Banner of Truth Trust, 1965.

Owen, John. *Of Communion with God the Father, Son, and Holy Ghost. In The Works of John Owen,* 2:1–274. Edited by William H. Goold. Edinburgh: Banner of Truth Trust, 1965.

Owen, John. *Of the Mortification of Sin in Believers.* In *The Works of John Owen,* 6:1–86. Edited by William H. Goold. Edinburgh: Banner of Truth Trust, 1967.

Secondary Sources

Barrett, Matthew and Michael Haykin. *John Owen on the Christian Life: Living for the Glory of God in Christ.* Wheaton, IL: Crossway, 2015.

Beeke, Joel and Mark Jones. "John Owen on Communion with the Triune God." In *A Puritan Theology: Doctrine for Life,* 101–16. Grand Rapids: Reformation Heritage Books, 2012.

Ferguson, Sinclair. *The Trinitarian Devotion of John Owen.* Orlando: Reformation Trust, 2014.

Trueman, Carl. *John Owen: Reformed Catholic, Renaissance Man.* Farnham, UK: Ashgate, 2007.

Christopher Love

Lesson Given by Geoff Thomas

Meditate

In one of her final letters before Christopher Love's execution, his wife wrote, "When the messenger of death comes to thee, let him not seem dreadful to thee, but look on him as a messenger that brings thee tidings of eternal life. When thou goest up the scaffold, think (as thou saidst to me) that it is but thy fiery chariot to carry thee up to thy Father's house." Meditate on Philippians 1:21.

Learn

John Gerstner once said, "High Calvinistic theology, meticulous discipline, and heart religion were providentially and sanctifyingly mixed together and out came Christopher Love." In this way, he became, as J. I. Packer called him, "a rising star in the world of Puritan ministry."

His Life

1618 Love is born in Cardiff, Wales.

1632 He is converted through the preaching of William Erbery.

1635 With the encouragement of Erbery, Love is admitted to New Inn Hall, Oxford, earning his bachelor's degree four years later.

1639 He moves to London where he becomes a chaplain to Sheriff Warner.

1640 Refusing ordination in the Anglican Church, Love goes to Scotland in pursuit of Presbyterian ordination. He is refused due to his desire to minister in England.

1641 Love returns to England only to be imprisoned for a sermon preached against the errors of the Church of England. Upon his release, he is made a chaplain at Windsor Castle.

1644 Love is ordained as a Presbyterian in London and begins to minister at St. Anne and St. Agnes, Aldersgate.

1645 He marries Ms. Mary Stone and completes his master's degree at Oxford.

1648 Love becomes a minister of St. Lawrence Jewry.

1651 Due to his alleged involvement in seeking to restore Charles II as the king of England, Love is arrested by Cromwell's forces. Just months later he is beheaded on Tower Hill, London.

Did You Know?

- Christopher Love had a great fondness of little ones and once told his wife, "If I had not been a preacher, I would have been content to teach children my whole life."

- When he was imprisoned in 1641, crowds would gather outside the prison gates to hear his convicting gospel preaching. It would take more than imprisonment to silence Love.

- Love was one of the youngest members of the Westminster Assembly, though his attendance was sporadic and infrequent.

- After his death, his wife, Mary, wrote of him, "He lived too much in heaven to live long out of heaven."

His Legacy

Christopher Love had a mind saturated with the realities of eternity which radically affected his marriage, preaching, and martyrdom.

The Momentariness of Marriage

Though Love never wrote on the subject of marriage, his relationship with Mary was a living sermon on the delight of a God-honoring marriage. He possessed an exclusive, superlative love for his bride. He wrote of her, "I dare not think that there is such a creature as Mary Love in the world." But he was also conscious that this marital joy was momentary and pointed forward to the bliss of heaven. His last words to his wife read, "Dear wife, farewell. I will call thee wife no more. I shall see thy face no more, yet I am not much troubled for now I am going to meet the Bridegroom, the Lord Jesus Christ, to whom I shall be eternally married."

The Terrors of Hell

In his work *Heaven's Glory, Hell's Terror*, Christopher Love devotes seven sermons to warn sinners of the eternal torment awaiting those outside of Christ. He writes, "Hell is a place of torment, ordained by God for Devils and reprobate sinners, wherein by his Justice he confines them to everlasting punishment; tormenting them both in Body and Soul, being deprived of God's favor, objects of his wrath, under which they must lie to all eternity." This vision of eternal woe, Love believed, ought to be proclaimed that men might turn from their sins and take refuge in Christ. To those who objected to his hell-fire preaching he said, "Sermons of terror have done more good upon unconverted souls than sermons of comfort have ever done."

The Blessedness of Martyrdom

The letters exchanged between Love and his friends, especially his wife, from the time of his arrest until his execution, reveal a man who counted it all joy to die for Christ. Love's last letter to Mary on the day of his beheading was titled "The Day of My Glorification." How could he view death with such hope? Turning to the sheriff on the execution block, he said, "I go from a block to the bosom of my Saviour." Love knew that the glory awaiting him was far better than anything this earth could offer him and counted it a great privilege to lay down his life for his Lord.

Reflect

1. Love's correspondence with his wife from Tower Hill indicates that he held loosely to the things of this earth, even the wife he loved so dearly. Are there people or possessions in your life that you cannot imagine losing? Do you cling to the things of this world? What is God's cure for the worldly soul?

2. Love regularly trafficked in the things of eternity. How often do you meditate upon the glories of heaven or the terrors of hell? Is your life characterized by a longing for and looking to the world to come?

3. Roger Drake, writing to Love just before his execution, stated, "Christ and His people are never more lovely than upon the cross." Such thinking is contrary to that of the world. Are you fearful of suffering reproach for Christ's sake? If so, why?

Discuss

1. Geoff Thomas relates how Love, having "never darkened the doors of a church," was marvelously converted through the preaching of God's Word. How central is the public preaching of the Scriptures in the fulfillment of the Great Commission? How does this affect our evangelism?

2. Love had multiple mentor-like figures in his life who discipled him and modeled biblical godliness before him. Why is mentoring so important in the life of the church? How does it foster spiritual growth in both the mentor and the one being mentored?

3. Mary, on the eve of Christopher's death, wrote to him, "Thy God will be our God and our portion. He will be a husband to thy widow and a father to thy children." She knew that through his death, Love would not only be ushered into Christ's presence, but she too would be kept by His love. How is the grace of Christ sufficient in our deepest sorrow and loss? Can you give an example of how Christ has demonstrated this in your own life?

4. While Christopher Love preached more on heaven, he was not afraid to compassionately tell his hearers of the wrath to come. How can "sermons of terror" be a source of great good to the hearts of sinners? Why is hell so little preached about today?

Read

___

Primary Sources

Love, Christopher. *The Dejected Soul's Cure*. Morgan, PA: Soli Deo Gloria, 2001.

Love, Christopher. *Grace: The Truth, Growth, and Different Degrees*. Morgan, PA: Soli Deo Gloria, 1997.

Love, Christopher. *The Penitent Pardoned*. Morgan, PA: Soli Deo Gloria, 2002.

Love, Christopher. *Preacher of God's Word: Sermons by Christopher Love*. Morgan, PA: Soli Deo Gloria, 2000.

Secondary Sources

Kistler, Don. *A Spectacle unto God: The Life and Death of Christopher Love*. Morgan, PA: Soli Deo Gloria, 1994.

John Bunyan

Lesson Given by Derek Thomas

Meditate

Bunyan wrote, "To see a prince entreat a beggar to receive an alms would be a strange sight; to see a king entreat a traitor to accept of mercy would be a stranger sight than that; but to see God entreat a sinner, to hear Christ say, 'I stand at the door and knock,' with a heart full and a heaven full of grace to bestow upon him that opens, this is such a sight as dazzles the eyes of angels." Meditate on 1 Peter 1:10–12.

Learn

His Life

1628   Bunyan is born in Elstow, England.

1644   After the death of his mother and sister, Bunyan runs away from home and joins Cromwell's New Model Army.

1651   Bunyan is introduced to John Gifford, a pastor in Bedford who leads him to repentance and faith.

1654   He moves to Bedford and becomes a member of Gifford's congregation, where he would quickly be appointed a deacon.

1655   Bunyan begins to gain popularity as a preacher of God's Word.

1660   He is arrested for preaching illegally, remaining in prison for twelve years.

1672   Bunyan is released from his first imprisonment and begins to pastor Bedford Baptist church.

1677   He is imprisoned a second time; during these six months in prison he finishes writing *The Pilgrim's Progress*.

1678   With the help of John Owen, Bunyan publishes part one of *The Pilgrim's Progress*.

1688   Bunyan dies suddenly from a fever caught while traveling in cold weather.

Did You Know?

- Prior to his conversion, while under deep conviction of sin, Bunyan confessed to be jealous of animals because they did not have a soul to account for before God.

- Bunyan's first imprisonment which lasted for twelve years was based upon no formal charge and no legal sentence. At points throughout this period, certain jailers permitted Bunyan to leave prison in order to preach.

- On his deathbed, Bunyan said to those who gathered around him, "Weep not for me, but for yourselves. I go to the Father of our Lord Jesus Christ, who will, no doubt, through the mediation of his blessed Son, receive me, though a sinner; where I hope we ere long shall meet, to sing the new song, and remain everlastingly happy, world without end."

- Bunyan's *The Pilgrim's Progress* sold more than 100,000 copies in its first decade in print and has since been reprinted in at least 1,500 editions and translated into more than two hundred languages.

His Legacy

John Bunyan was an exemplary pilgrim, possessing no lasting city here, but seeking the city which is to come (Heb. 13:14). There is much we can learn from him about living as a stranger in this present world.

The Pilgrim's Sufferings

While life in prison was full of hardship for Bunyan, nothing caused him greater pain than being separated from his wife and children, especially his blind daughter. He described it as a "pulling of the flesh from my bones" which "[broke] my heart to pieces." Understanding his pilgrim identity, however, enabled Bunyan to suffer with joy for Christ's sake. After quoting 2 Corinthians 1:9, Bunyan wrote, "By this scripture I was made to see that if ever I would suffer rightly, I must first pass a sentence of death upon everything that can be properly called a thing of this life, even to reckon myself, my wife, my children, my health, my enjoyment, and all, as dead to me, and myself as dead to them. The second was, to live upon God that is invisible, as Paul said in another place; the way not to faint, is to 'look not at the things which are seen, but at the things which are not seen; for the things which are seen are temporal, but the things which are not seen are eternal.'"

The Pilgrim's Perseverance

In *The Pilgrim's Progress*, Bunyan portrays the Christian life as a long and difficult journey, strewn with temptation and opposition. The pilgrim's final destination, of course, is the Celestial City, but in order to get there, great perseverance is required. While the true Christian is preserved by the grace of Christ, there is yet a need for him to strive with all of his might to enter the kingdom of God. Bunyan wrote, "This is Christ, who continually with the oil of his grace, maintains the work already began in the heart. You see, a prevailing view of God's grace does understand that ultimately we persevere because Jesus is working in us, but it doesn't do so without extraordinary effort and a mindfulness of the consequences of apostasy." Without such a diligent striving and persistent believing, we will not reach our heavenly rest (Heb. 4:1).

The Pilgrim's Company

Bunyan was tireless in stressing that the Christian life is not an individualistic one. In *The Pilgrim's Progress*, Christian is in the constant company of others. He is shown the way of life through Evangelist, travels with Faithful at his side until Faithful's martyrdom, and then is accompanied by Hopeful to the end. There are also numerous other characters who assist Christian on his journey. Through this, Bunyan teaches us that the pilgrim journey is to be made in the context of the local church. It is not only the grace of Christ which enables us to persevere but the body of Christ, as Christians encourage and exhort one another in the faith. Bunyan illustrates this beautifully when he writes of Christian and Faithful: "I saw in my dream that both of them went on very lovingly together; and they had delightful conversation about all of the things that had happened to them on their pilgrimage." Pilgrims are not meant to journey alone.

Reflect

1. What does it look like to view the world through the eyes of a pilgrim? How does one "live upon God that is invisible"?

2. Derek Thomas says that Bunyan referred to the Bible as a mirror, a map, and a sword. How ought the Scriptures to function in these three ways in your own life?

3. How have brothers and sisters in Christ been used to strengthen your faith? In what ways could you intentionally seek to encourage others in your church as they journey toward their heavenly home?

Discuss

1. What is the relationship between suffering and heavenly mindedness? How do tribulations promote a pilgrim mentality? And how does a pilgrim mentality enable us to endure tribulations?

2. How do divine preservation and human perseverance relate? Why does the doctrine of God's preservation of His children not nullify the need for them to persevere in the faith?

3. Why is Christian fellowship so essential to the Christian life? What means has God given for Christians to encourage one another in the faith?

4. What lessons can we learn from Bunyan's lack of education? Is there a place for ministers who have no formal education?

Read

_____

Primary Sources

Bunyan, John. *Grace Abounding.* Edinburgh: Banner of Truth Trust, 2018.

Bunyan, John. *The Pilgrim's Progress.* Edinburgh: Banner of Truth Trust, 2017.

Bunyan, John. *The Works of John Bunyan.* 3 volumes. Edinburgh: Banner of Truth Trust, 1999.

Secondary Sources

Beeke, Joel and Paul Smalley. *John Bunyan and the Grace of Fearing God.* Phillipsburg, NJ: Presbyterian & Reformed, 2016.

Cook, Faith. *A Pilgrim Path: John Bunyan's Journey.* Darlington, England: Evangelical Press, 2017.

Greaves, Richard. *John Bunyan and English Nonconformity.* London: Hambledon Press, 1992.

John Flavel

Lesson Given by Brian Cosby

Meditate

John Flavel said, "To depend partly upon Christ's righteousness, and partly upon our own, is to set one foot upon a rock, and the other in a quick-sand; either Christ will be to us all in all, or nothing at all, in point of righteousness and salvation.... As he did the whole *work*, so he expects the whole *praise*; if he be not able to save to the uttermost, why do we depend upon him at all? And if he be, why do we lean upon any beside him?" Meditate on Romans 4:1–8.

Learn

Isaac Watts praised Flavel as "that most excellent, practical, and evangelical writer." James W. Alexander wrote, "To my taste, Flavel is the most uniformly interesting, engaging, and refreshing writer on religion, ancient or modern."

His Life

1628   Flavel is born around this time in Bromsgrove, Worcestershire,
to Richard Flavel, a Presbyterian minister.

1650   He is ordained by the presbytery at Salisbury, becoming the pastor of a
congregation in Diptford.

1656   Flavel accepts a call to be minister in the thriving seaport of Dartmouth.

1662   He is ejected from the pulpit for nonconformity, but he continues to
meet secretly with his church members for worship.

1665   Due to the Five Mile Act, Flavel moves to Slapton, persisting in
preaching and ministering to his people.

1672   He returns to Dartmouth after an indulgence is passed giving
Nonconformists freedom to worship.

1673   When this indulgence is canceled, Flavel carries on his ministry in
secret, mainly through writing.

1682   Flavel is forced to seek safety in London, assisting there in the
congregation of a friend.

1684   He returns to Dartmouth where his ministry is confined to his home.

1687   An indulgence is issued, allowing Flavel to preach publicly once again.

1691   Flavel dies, having suffered from a massive stroke in Exeter.

Did You Know?

- Though providing a smaller income, Flavel accepted the call to minister in the thriving seaport of Dartmouth because he believed he would be more useful to the Lord there.

- On one occasion, Flavel disguised himself as a woman on horseback in order to reach a secret meeting place to preach and administer baptism.

- Flavel was a man of great learning who had a working knowledge of English, Latin, French, Greek, Hebrew, Chaldean, Syriac, and Arabic.

- Near the end of his ministry in Dartmouth, a mob burned an effigy (i.e., a representation) of him, showing their deep hatred toward his ministry. But he pressed on, praying for his beloved Dartmouth, "O that there were not a prayerless family in this town!"

His Legacy

John Flavel's best-selling book was entitled *Keeping the Heart or A Saint Indeed*. From 1668 to 1800 it went through 41 printings and continues to be used by the Lord today to bring many into a more intentional pursuit of holiness. Based upon Proverbs 4:23, Flavel taught that "the keeping and the right managing of the heart in every condition, is the great business of a Christian's life." Since it is from the heart that the springs of life flow, there is nothing that could be more important than a vigilant watching over, maintaining, and cultivating of the heart. Flavel said, "The heart of man is his worst part before it is regenerated, and the best afterwards. It is the seat of principles and foundation of actions. The eye of God is, and the eye of the Christian ought to be, principally fixed upon it."

Keeping-the-Heart Defined

But what does it mean to keep the heart? Keeping the heart, wrote Flavel, is "nothing else but the constant care and diligence of such a renewed man, to preserve his soul in that holy frame to which grace hath reduced it, and daily strives to hold it." In other words, this great task of keeping the heart entails a careful watchfulness which is ever mortifying sin and cultivating grace and godliness in Christ. The great goal of such heart-keeping is to foster "actual fellowship or communion...with Christ in holy duties, wherein Christians let forth their hearts to God by desires, and God lets forth his comforts and refreshments into their hearts." For Flavel, this was the very marrow of the Christian life.

Keeping-the-Heart Required

The Christian must be constantly at the work of keeping his heart. "The heart is a hungry and restless thing," Flavel explained, "it will have something to feed upon; if it enjoy nothing from God, it will hunt for something among the creatures, and there it often loses itself, as well as its end...that which we delight in we are never weary of." If the heart be not regularly examined, if it be not kept in a holy frame, if the lusts of the flesh be not mortified, if the graces of godliness be not intentionally pursued, then the Christian will find himself in a woeful condition and be of little use to God. Without such a work, wrote Flavel, "all other duties are of no value to God."

Keeping-the-Heart Pursued

While it is the principle work of the Christian, keeping the heart is also a most difficult work: "You find in the Word, a world of work cut out for Christians; there is hearing-work, praying-work, reading, meditating, and self-examining work; it puts him also upon a constant watch over all the corruptions of his heart. Oh, what a world of work hath a Christian about him?" This work is to be carried out by a frequent examination of the heart, humble repentance for heart-sin, ardent prayer for purifying grace, close study and meditation of the Scriptures, and constant awareness of God's presence.

Reflect

1. Read Proverbs 4:23. What is the condition of your heart? What reason does Solomon give for vigilantly keeping the heart?

2. Flavel wrote, "God doth not usually indulge lazy and negligent hearts with the comforts of assurance; He will not so much as seem to patronize sloth and carelessness." What is the relationship between keeping your heart and possessing assurance of salvation?

3. Flavel called the Christian to maintain "a constant holy jealousy" over his own heart. Do you have such a jealousy? If not, what are the reasons for your indifference toward your spiritual condition?

Discuss

1. What does "the heart" refer to in Scripture? Why is it so central in biblical religion?

2. "Above all other studies in the world, study your own hearts," said Flavel. In what ways does this statement need to be qualified? How does one avoid morbid introspection when seeking to understand his own heart?

3. What are the fruits of a well-kept heart? If the benefits of keeping the heart are so great, why are we so prone to negligence in this area?

4. Flavel's life was characterized by much outward instability, with three wives dying and frequent persecution. What enabled him to maintain a healthy inward stability of soul throughout all the ups and downs of life?

Read

Primary Sources

Flavel, John. *The Works of John Flavel.* 6 volumes. Edinburgh: Banner of Truth Trust, 1968.

Flavel, John. *The Mystery of Providence.* Edinburgh: Banner of Truth Trust, 1976.

Flavel, John. *Keeping the Heart.* Fearn, UK: Christian Focus, 2012.

Secondary Sources

Cosby, Brian. *John Flavel: Puritan Life and Thought in Stuart England.* Lanham, MD: Lexington Books, 2013.

Embry, Adam. *Keeper of the Great Seal of Heaven: Sealing of the Spirit in the Life and Thought of John Flavel.* Grand Rapids: Reformation Heritage Books, 2011.

Yuille, J. Stephen. *The Inner Sanctum of Puritan Piety: John Flavel's Doctrine of Mystical Union with Christ.* Grand Rapids: Reformation Heritage Books, 2007.

Matthew Henry

Lesson Given by William VanDoodewaard

Meditate

Matthew Henry wrote, "Let not self, carnal self, be the spring and centre of your prayers, but God; let the eye of the soul be fixed upon him as your highest end in all your applications to him; let this be the habitual disposition of your souls, to be to your God for a name and a praise; and let this be your design in all your desires, that God may be glorified, and by this let them all be directed, determined, sanctified, and, when need is, overruled." Meditate on Matthew 6:9–10.

Learn

His Life

1662   Henry is born on October 18, to Puritan minister Philip Henry.

1672   Somewhere in this period, Henry is converted.

1680   He studies under Thomas Doolittle at Islington.

1685   Henry, with little hope of being called into the ministry, begins to study law at Gray's Inn.

1687   His gifts being clearly evidenced, Henry is secretly ordained in London and begins to minister in Chester. Shortly thereafter, he marries Katherine Hardware.

1690   After the death of Katherine, Henry marries Mary Warburton.

1704   He begins working on his *magnum opus* titled *Exposition of the Old and New Testaments.*

1712   Henry accepts a call to move to Hackney to minister in one of the most prominent congregations near London.

1714   Henry dies on his way home from visiting Cheshire, having fallen from his horse.

1721   The final volume of his commentary is published, his notes and writings on Romans through Revelation being compiled by Henry's friends.

Did You Know?

- Though born prematurely and physically frail as a child, Henry evidenced a profound spirituality and intellectual ability from a very young age.

- Every Lord's Day, Henry would lecture on the Old Testament in the morning (before the morning sermon) and the New Testament in the afternoon. By the end of his ministry in Cheshire, he had taken his congregation through the whole Bible two times!

- In addition to his congregational work and publishing endeavors, Henry held monthly services at five neighboring villages and regularly preached to prisoners in the castle.

- Henry wrote a biography of his father, Philip Henry, which Thomas Chalmers called "one of the most precious religious biographies in our language."

His Legacy

Matthew Henry has, through his writings, left the church a rich legacy of biblical spirituality. But perhaps nothing he wrote has had a more far-reaching impact on the church than his *Exposition of the Old and New Testaments* and his *Method of Prayer*. These two great works take us to the heart of Henry's life and ministry, teaching us that Christianity is characterized by whole-Bible exposition and whole-souled prayer.

Whole-Bible Exposition

"As long as the Bible continues in England," wrote William Tong, "Mr. Henry's admirable *Expositions* will be prized by all serious Christians; in them his clear head, his warm heart, his life, his soul appears." Henry's ministry was governed by a passion to see the whole of the Bible understood, believed, and experientially applied to God's people. He labored tirelessly in the pulpit and with his pen toward this end. "It is better to be without bread in your houses than without Bibles," Henry said, "for the words of God's mouth are and should be to you more than any necessary food." Before beginning his commentary, Henry set forth six principles which grounded his work:

1. That religion is the one thing needful.

2. That divine revelation is necessary to true religion.

3. That divine revelation is not now to be found nor expected anywhere but in the Scriptures of the Old and New Testament.

4. That the Scriptures of the Old and New Testaments were purposely designed for our learning.

5. That the Holy Scriptures were not only designed for our learning, but are the settled standing rule for our faith and practice.

6. That therefore it is the duty of all Christians diligently to search the Scriptures, and it is the office of ministers to guide and assist them therein.

The whole Bible is profitable and most necessary in the Christian's pursuit of godliness. Henry enjoins us, "Grow upwards in heavenly mindedness, downward in humility. Be pressing forward. The way to grow in grace is to use what we have. The Word is the means of our growth. Make daily use of it (2 Tim. 3.17)."

Whole-Souled Prayer

Matthew Henry labored not only to help God's people understand their Bibles, but also to help them to deepen their communion with God through prayer. His *Method of Prayer* follows the pattern of adoration, confession of sin, petition for ourselves, thanksgiving, intercession for others, and a conclusion. Every point in his work includes Scripture after Scripture woven together as possible expressions of prayer. He sought to fill the mouth of God's people with God's own words, writing, "God's word must be the guide of your desires and the ground of your expectations in prayer." For Henry there was nothing more wonderful in this life than walking with God in prayer. He said, "This life of communion with God, and constant attendance upon him, is a heaven upon earth."

Reflect

1. Read 2 Timothy 3:16. Are there certain portions of Scripture that you tend to avoid, thinking them unprofitable? What changes could you make to ensure that you are feeding on all 66 books of the Bible on an annual or biannual basis?

2. Henry wrote, "And in every prayer remember you are speaking to God, and make it to appear you have an awe of him upon your spirits." Is your prayer life pervaded with a sense of God's majesty and holiness? Why must all of our prayers ultimately be prayers of adoration?

3. "I love prayer," wrote Henry in his diary. "It is that which buckles on all the Christian's armour." Do you love prayer? How does a love for prayer evidence a love for God?

Discuss

———

1. What lessons can the church learn today from Henry's devotion to the whole canon of Scripture? How ought the church, through its preaching, teaching, and discipleship, seek to foster a love for the whole of Scripture among its members?

2. Why is a healthy Christian a whole-Bible Christian? What is the role of Scripture in the Christian's sanctification?

3. Henry's method of prayer entailed adoration, confession, petition, thanksgiving, and intercession. Would you change the order or add any elements? In which of these areas do you need to improve?

4. "When God intends great mercy for His people," said Henry, "the first thing He does is set them a-praying." Why is this ordinarily the case? What does this teach us about the centrality of prayer in the life of the church?

Read

Primary Sources

Henry, Matthew. *Commentary on the Whole Bible.* 6 volumes. Peabody, MA: Hendrickson Publishers, 1991.

Henry, Matthew. *A Method for Prayer.* Edited by J. Ligon Duncan III. Fearn, UK: Christian Focus, 1994.

Henry, Matthew. *The Complete Works of Matthew Henry.* 2 volumes. Grand Rapids: Baker, 1997.

Secondary Sources

Harman, Allan. *Matthew Henry: His Life and Influence.* Fearn, UK: Christian Focus, 2012.

Eveson, Philip. *Matthew Henry.* Darlington, England: Evangelical Press, 2012.

Beeke, Joel and Mark Jones. "Matthew Henry on a Practical Method of Daily Prayer." In *A Puritan Theology: Doctrine for Life*, 877–87. Grand Rapids: Reformation Heritage Books, 2012.

American Puritans

Lesson Given by Stephen Nichols

Meditate

Once when threatened by a Native American with a knife, John Eliot retorted, "I am about the work of the great God, and he is with me, so that I fear not all the sachems [chiefs] of the country. I'll go on, and do you touch me if you dare." Meditate on Matthew 10:28.

Learn

Their Lives

John Eliot (1604–1690): pastor of the Roxbury church for nearly 60 years, missionary to the Native Americans, and translator of the Bible into Algonquin.

John Davenport (1597–1670): pastor and cofounder of the colony of Quinnipiac, which was later renamed New Haven.

John Tennent (1707–1732): son of William Tennent and minister of Old Scots Church in New Jersey for only two years due to an untimely death.

John Brainerd (1720–1781): missionary to the Native Americans at Bethel, New Jersey, for 33 years in the place of his deceased brother David Brainerd.

John Wauwaumpequunnaunt: Mohican translator for John Sergeant, Timothy Woodbridge, and Jonathan Edwards at Stockbridge, Massachusetts.

Did You Know?

- Only two of John Eliot's six children outlived him. He once commented on this, "My desire was that they should have served God on earth; but if God will choose to have them rather in heaven, I have nothing to object against it, but his will be done!"

- John Davenport was invited to participate in the Westminster Assembly in 1643, but decided to continue ministering in New Haven instead.

- A biographer of John Brainerd wrote of him, "He was a lover of all good men and seems to have hated nothing but sin; he was a holy man of God, to which his whole life bore witness."

- Jonathan Edwards held his interpreter John Wauwaumpequunnaunt in the highest esteem, calling him "an extraordinary man on some accounts" and considering him to possibly be the most scripturally learned Native American in the colonies. One can only imagine having spent seven years translating Edwards's sermons!

Their Legacy

The five Johns of American Puritanism, though unknown to many today, serve as shining examples of vibrant Christianity.

Missional Evangelism

Through translating the Word into the native tongue (Eliot), founding an American colony upon the Word (Davenport), proclaiming the Word from the pulpit (Tennent and Brainerd), and translating the preached Word (Wauwaumpequunnaunt), these men evidenced a passion for the Scriptures and for making the true God known to lost mankind. They were zealous in evangelism, seeking to bring the gospel to people whom it had never reached before. God blessed their labors, using them to advance His kingdom on the American frontier. Jonathan Edwards wrote of John Brainerd's ministry, "We have had accounts from time to time of religion being in a flourishing state in the Indian congregation of New Jersey, under the care of Mr. John Brainerd; of the congregation's increasing by the access of Indians from distant places; of a work of awakening being carried on among the unconverted, and of additions made to the number of the hopefully converted."

Educational Promotion

These men were passionate about education, striving to establish sound academic institutions. Eliot actively set up schools in the native towns. To help in the schools, he published *The Indian Grammar Begun* (1666), *The Indian Primer* (1669), and *The Logic Primer* (1672). A building was even erected for an "Indian college" at Harvard. Davenport also helped in the formation of Harvard College and had dreams of establishing such a school in New Haven. These dreams were met after his death in the 1701 founding of Yale University. John Tennent's father, William, had founded a classical school, which would come to be Princeton University. Along with these men, Wauwaumpequunnaunt translated for Timothy Woodbridge, in efforts to teach the natives how to read and write. We learn from these American Puritans the importance of Christian education.

Persevering Faithfulness

All of these men labored diligently in the work which God gave them to do. But, as Stephen Nichols points out, the hard-working persistence of John Eliot stands out above the rest. He labored tirelessly to see the gospel go forth in Roxbury, serving the Lord for nearly sixty years. Along with his extensive preaching ministry, he was an avid translator, seeking to get as much biblical literature into the hands of the Native Americans as he possibly could. He not only translated the entire Bible into the Algonquin language but also translated classics of Puritan piety, grammars, and catechisms. He established fourteen towns of "praying Indians," wherein there were approximately 1,100 Native American Christians. But because of King Philip's War in 1675, these towns were wiped out. Eliot labored until his dying day to see them reestablished, but was not successful. In his final days, he said, "The Lord revive and prosper that work, and grant it may live when I am dead. It is a work, which I have been doing much and long about. But what was the word I spoke last? I recall that word, 'my doings.' Alas, they have been poor and small and lean doings, and I'll be the man that shall throw the first stone at them all." Eliot exuded a profound humility as he looked back upon the zealous labors of his hands.

Reflect

1. Nichols suggests that the lives of these five men were governed by their doctrine of God (i.e., their understanding of who God is). Is your life dominated by a vision of the sovereign, gracious, triune God? In other words, do you fear God? How could you practically cultivate such reverential fear?

2. Each of these men were radically devoted to the Scriptures, seeking to live by them and propagate them in the world. How would you describe your relation to the Bible? Do you have a genuine love and passion for the Scriptures and a desire to share its truth with others?

3. By the end of John Eliot's life, there was little remaining of his once very prosperous ministry among the Native Americans. Yet he labored just as faithfully and diligently in his later years as he did in the former. Are you willing to serve the Lord ardently in your vocation even if He doesn't externally bless your labors? Is it your aim to please Him even if it means you will look like a failure to the world?

Discuss

1. Many object to Calvinism, saying that it stifles missionary zeal, but clearly Brainerd and Eliot, both self-professing Calvinists, would have thought otherwise. How does a belief in the sovereignty of God's grace actually promote passion for missions? Why evangelize if God has already determined whom He will save?

2. What does the self-sacrificing love of Eliot and Brainerd toward the Native Americans teach us about racism? How does the gospel deal a death blow to such sinful prejudice?

3. These men represent the wider Puritan conviction of the importance of sound education. Why did they exercise as much zeal in establishing schools as they did churches? What is the relationship between strong education and a healthy church?

4. Eliot's final words, "Welcome joy!" lead us to "the heart of Puritanism," says Nichols. How is this the case? What would you say is the heart of Puritanism?

Read

Clark, Michael P, ed. *The Eliot Tracts: With Letters from John Eliot to Thomas Thorowgood and Richard Baxter.* Santa Barbara, CA: Greenwood Press, 2003.

Hall, David D. *A Reforming People: Puritanism and the Transformation of Public Life in New England.* New York: Alfred A Knopf, 2011.

Gray, Kathryn N. *John Eliot and the Praying Indians of Massachusetts Bay: Communities and Connections in Puritan New England.* Lewisburg, PA: Bucknell University Press, 2013.

Edwards, Jonathan. *The Life and Diary of David Brainerd.* Grand Rapids: Baker, 1989.

Jonathan Edwards

Lesson Given by Joe Rigney

Meditate

Joe Rigney quoted Edwards as saying, "The enjoyment of God is the only happiness with which our souls can be satisfied." Meditate on Psalm 16:11.

Learn

Samuel Davies referred to Edwards as "the profoundest reasoner, and the greatest divine...that America ever produced." Though Edwards was extremely gifted intellectually, John De Witt contends that "he was greatest in his attribute of regnant, permeating, irradiating spirituality."

His Life

1703 Edwards is born in East Windsor, Connecticut, to Timothy Edwards and Esther Stoddard.

1721 He is converted through the reading of 1 Timothy 1:17, by which "a sense of the glory of the Divine Being" flooded his soul.

1722 Edwards begins his ministerial career in a Presbyterian church in New York City.

1723 He completes his master's degree at Yale and becomes the minister of a church in Bolton.

1724 Edwards returns to New Haven to serve as tutor at the college.

1726 He receives a call to assist his grandfather, Solomon Stoddard, in the church in Northampton, Massachusetts, becoming the sole minister two years later after Stoddard's death.

1727 He marries Sarah Pierrepont shortly after settling in Northampton.

1734 Edwards's ministry in Northampton is blessed with multiple revivals described in his work *Faithful Narrative of Surprising Conversions*.

1740 Edwards is instrumentally used by God in the propagation and defense of the Great Awakening.

1750 Due to doctrinal disagreements and various discipline cases, the members of Northampton vote to eject Edwards from the pulpit.

1751 He becomes a pastor to a small congregation and a missionary to the Housatonic Indians in Stockbridge.

1758 Edwards accepts the call as president of the College of New Jersey at Princeton. However, he dies shortly thereafter due to complications from a small pox vaccination.

Did You Know?

- Edwards's grandfather, Solomon Stoddard, pastored the same church for sixty years, and his father Timothy Edwards pastored the same congregation for fifty-six years. Both men were powerful preachers and no strangers to religious revivals.

- When his work permitted, Edwards would spend thirteen hours a day in his study. This would have been normal for most professions of that time and enabled him to produce the vast body of writings that he did.

- On July 8, 1741, Edwards preached his famous sermon, "Sinners in the Hands of an Angry God." A witness said, "Before the sermon was done, there was a great moaning and crying out throughout the whole house. What shall I do to be saved?" Edwards was unable to complete his sermon because of the uproar.

- Just after Edwards's unexpected death, Sarah Edwards wrote, "What shall I say? A holy and good God has covered us with a dark cloud. O that we may kiss the rod, and lay our hands on our mouths! The Lord has done it.... My God lives; and he has my heart."

His Legacy

Rigney asserts that the glorification of the triune God as the goal of creation and redemption was "the animating principle of all of Edwards's ministry, all of his life, all of his practice."

The Uniqueness of God's Glory

Edwards's thought was pervaded by the unique and incomprehensible glory of God. In a sermon titled "God's Excellencies," he said, "God is infinitely exalted above all created beings." Expounding upon various attributes of God, Edwards showed how the Lord is in a category all His own. This clear distinction between the all-glorious Creator and His image-bearing creatures was of fundamental significance for Edwards.

With the rise of the man-centered thinking of the Enlightenment, he championed a God-centered and God-exalting worldview.

The Enjoyment of God's Glory

Edwards stressed that God communicates Himself to His creatures not only so that His glory might be known intellectually but so that it might be enjoyed affectionately. He writes, "God is glorified not only by His glory being seen, but by its being rejoiced in. When those who see it delight in it, God is more glorified than if they only see it." God invites His creatures to share in the joyous fellowship that exists between the three persons of the Trinity. And how could this be experienced without profound delight? For Edwards, there could be no divorcing of head and heart in the Christian life.

The Pervasiveness of God's Glory

Edwards saw his glorious God everywhere he turned his eyes. First, he believed God's glory to be supremely revealed upon the pages of Holy Scripture. Second, he saw the revelation of God's glory in nature. From spiders to chocolate, everything revealed something of God's grandeur as the Creator. And third, he beheld God's glory in the events of human history. In every age, nothing came to pass apart from the divine will. For Edwards, all things in Scripture, nature, and history pertained to and had their end in the glory of God.

Reflect

1. Edwards's life was clearly fueled by a passion for God's glory. What motivates you? Is your chief aim in life to make much of God?

2. Edwards perceived the danger of a knowledge void of affections and affections void of knowledge. In your pursuit of God, are you more prone to neglect the head or the heart? What negative effects does this have on your spirituality and how could you remedy it?

3. Do you regularly delight in the glory of God as it is revealed in history? How does viewing history in a God-centered way deliver from fear and inspire hope?

Discuss

1. The Apostle Paul tells us that we are to glorify God in all that we do, even in the minutest details of our daily existence (1 Cor. 10:31). What does it mean to glorify God? And how do we practically live toward this end?

2. Martyn Lloyd-Jones refers to Edwards as "pre-eminently the theologian of revival." What is true revival? How has the concept of revival been corrupted throughout church history? Should we be pursuing revival today? If so, how?

3. How is God's glory revealed in the Scriptures and how does one come to see it? What is the relation of God's revelation in Scripture to His revelation in nature and history?

4. Rigney referenced Edwards's use of "natural typology," which sees images of the divine in created things. What are some examples of this? How do we avoid extremes in viewing the world in this way?

Read

Primary Sources

Edwards, Jonathan. *The Works of Jonathan Edwards*. 2 volumes. Edinburgh: Banner of Truth Trust, 1974. (Also, see The Works of Jonathan Edwards. 26 volumes. New Haven, CT: Yale University Press, 1957–2006).

Edwards, Jonathan. *Altogether Lovely: Jonathan Edwards on the Glory and Excellency of Jesus Christ*. Morgan, PA: Soli Deo Gloria, 1998.

Edwards, Jonathan. *Our Great and Glorious God*. Morgan, PA: Soli Deo Gloria, 2003.

Secondary Sources

Murray, Iain. *Johnathan Edwards: A New Biography*. Edinburgh: Banner of Truth Trust, 1987.

Marsden, George. *Jonathan Edwards: A Life*. New Haven, CT: Yale University Press, 2003.

Piper, John and Justin Taylor, eds. *A God-Entranced Vision of All Things: The Legacy of Jonathan Edwards*. Wheaton, IL: Crossway, 2004.

Puritan Women: Katherine Willoughby & Anne Bradstreet

Lesson Given by Michael Haykin and Joel Beeke

Meditate

Anne Bradstreet, the great poet of Puritanism, expressed her longing for eternity:

Oh how I long to be at rest
    and soar on high among the blest.
This body shall in silence sleep
    mine eyes no more shall ever weep.
No fainting fits shall me assail
    nor grinding pains my body frail.
With cares and fears ne'r cumbred be
    nor losses know, nor sorrows see.

Meditate on Revelation 21:2–4.

Learn

Their Lives

1519   Willoughby is born in 1519 to a prominent Roman Catholic family.

1540   Somewhere in this period Willoughby becomes convinced of Reformation truth.

1553   After Mary ascends the throne, Willoughby flees England, seeking refuge in the Netherlands.

1557   Willoughby is invited to Poland, where her husband would become a leading political figure in Lithuania.

1559   Willoughby returns to England after Elizabeth is crowned Queen, where she would pursue reform for the rest of her days.

1580   On September 19, Katherine Willoughby dies.

1612   Bradstreet is born to Dorothy and Thomas Dudley in Northampton, England.

1628   At the young age of 16, she marries Simon Bradstreet.

1630   Bradstreet boards the *Arbella* to sail to the New World with her family in pursuit of religious freedom.

1650   Without her consent, Bradstreet's poetry was submitted to a publisher in London by her brother-in-law.

1672   Bradstreet dies, leaving her husband and children behind.

Did You Know?

- In 1551, after her husband's death six years earlier, Willoughby lost both of her sons due to the sweating sickness (a fatal illness) within an hour of each other. This trial was used of the Lord to strengthen her faith and boldness in the cause of Christ.

- Willoughby used her wealth to publish many Reformation works in England, including those of William Tyndale and Hugh Latimer.

- Upon reading the first publication of her work, Bradstreet was very displeased by the number of errors made by the printer. The second edition with her corrections and additions, however, would not be published until six years after her death.

- Bradstreet, no stranger to hardship, once told her children, "If at any time you are chastened of God, take it as thankfully and joyfully as in greatest mercies, for if ye be his ye shall reap the greatest benefit by it."

Their Legacy

Willoughby and Bradstreet are shining examples of the many fearless, wise, and gracious women who labored during the Puritan era.

Women of Bold Bravery

Both of these women possessed a feminine strength and courage in the cause of Christ. Forsaking the comforts and pleasures of this earthly life, they evidenced a willingness to die for the sake of Reformation truth. Willoughby displayed a boldness and bravery as she stood against anti-reformation monarchs such as "Bloody" Mary and religious figures such as Bishop Gardiner. Forfeiting wealth and prestige and being forced to flee from her beloved England, she was unremittent in her promotion of biblical religion. Bradstreet, unwilling to succumb to religious compromise, boarded a ship for the New World, not knowing what might lie ahead. These Puritan women teach us that true femininity is not weak, but tough and heroic in Christ's service.

Women of Penetrating Intellect

Bradstreet labored to understand Scripture and used her poetry as a means to meditate upon and share its profound truths with others. While her literary work was well received, the fact that it was penned by a woman was met with surprise and ridicule. One of her critics, Nathaniel Ward, characterized the common thinking of the day when he claimed that women have "squirrel brains." Challenging this idea of the intellectual inferiority of women, Bradstreet wrote, "Let such as say our Sex is void of Reason, / Know, tis a Slander now, but once was Treason." Heidi Nichols writes of Bradstreet, "While she felt compelled to deprecate her own abilities, partly due to the literary conventions of the day, she took issue with those who disregarded her work simply due to her gender." She rightly fought against the false notion that women ought not to meddle in intellectual affairs because they are somehow of lesser ability than men.

Katherine Willoughby was also a public promoter of Reformation doctrine, showing herself to be a careful theologian who could hold her own in theological debate. She supported many of the leading figures in the cause of the English Reformation, using her status, wit, and wealth to spread the truth of God.

Women of Domestic Devotion

While these women were not afraid to labor for the cause of God outside of their homes, they were also exemplary wives and mothers. Having lost her husband and both sons by 1551, Willoughby married one of her servants, Richard Bertie, in 1553. They would have a happy marriage together despite the turmoil and persecution they faced for their Reformation faith. Katherine, while active in the promotion of English Protestantism, remained diligent in keeping the home and training the children.

Marrying at the age of sixteen, Bradstreet would also love and assist her husband, Simon, until her dying day. She poetically described her devotion to her eight children: "I had eight birds hatched in one nest, / four cocks there were, and hens the rest. / I nursed them up with pain and care, / nor cost, nor labor did I spare, / till at the last they felt their wing, / mounted the trees and learnt to sing." Far from neglecting their domestic duties, these women gave themselves whole-heartedly to their families, while still making time to promote gospel truth outside of the home.

Reflect

1. Willoughby and Bradstreet teach us that Christianity is marked by a certain toughness of soul. Read 2 Timothy 2:3. Do you think of yourself as a soldier in the ranks of Christ? How does such an identity prepare you to suffer for Him?

2. Michael Haykin spoke of Willoughby's frustration due to the "snail-pace" of the Reformation under Queen Elizabeth. Are you patient, prayerful, and diligent with others when the work of God in them progresses more slowly than you would like? Why does the Lord often perform His work at a "snail-pace"?

3. Both Willoughby and Bradstreet rightly prioritized their families, even while using their gifts to serve the broader church and world. Is your life rightly prioritized? Why is it so easy to neglect our primary duties for the sake of other things?

1. Willoughby and Bradstreet had specific crosses to bear in their day which necessitated great bravery. How does a Christian cultivate such strength of soul in order to ensure readiness to suffer for Christ's sake?

2. In many ways, the inferiority of women in Bradstreet's day is the opposite of the feminism which characterizes twenty-first century America. How does the biblical view of womanhood address the errors of both the seventeenth century and our own?

3. Why is poetry such a helpful vehicle for communicating biblical truth?

4. What do these ladies teach us about the church's pursuit of reformation? What specific lessons can women today draw from their examples in the promotion of biblical truth?

Read

Primary Sources

Bradstreet, Anne. *The Complete Works of Anne Bradstreet.* Cambridge, MA: Belknap Press, 1981.

Bradstreet, Anne. *To My Husband and Other Poems.* Mineola, NY: Dover Publications, 2000.

Secondary Sources

VanDoodewaard, Rebecca. *Reformation Women: Sixteenth-Century Figures Who Shaped Christianity's Rebirth,* 81–89. Grand Rapids: Reformation Heritage Books, 2017.

Nichols, Heidi. Anne Bradstreet: *A Guided Tour of the Life and Thought of a Puritan Poet.* Phillipsburg, NJ: Presbyterian & Reformed, 2006.

Cook, Faith. Anne Bradstreet: *Pilgrim and Poet.* Darlington, England: Evangelical Press, 2010.

PART TWO
Puritan-Minded Figures

Dutch "Puritans": Gisbertus Voetius & Wilhemus à Brakel

Lesson Given by Joel Beeke

Meditate

A key word in Voetius's vocabulary of the Christian life was "precision," which he defined as "the exact or perfect human action conforming to the law of God as taught by God, and genuinely accepted, intended, and desired by believers." Meditate on Ephesians 5:15.

Learn

Gisbertus Voetius and Wilhelmus à Brakel were two of the most influential pastors, theologians, and authors in the Dutch Further Reformation. A eulogy of Voetius states, "Few men have in any age exercised greater influence over the church of their time and country." Abraham Hellenbroak said of Brakel's systematic theology, "No family should be without it: the fruit which it has borne everywhere, and still bears, is extraordinary: from far and near one hears of the most lofty and remarkable testimonies."

Their Lives

1589   Voetius is born at Heusden, the Netherlands, to a godly family
        of Reformed persuasion.

1611   After many years of studying theology, Voetius is ordained and begins
        ministering at Vlijmen.

1618   Voetius is appointed a member of the international Synod of Dort
        despite his youth.

1634   Voetius becomes a professor in the new Academy of Utrecht, where he
        would teach for forty-two years until his death.

1635   Brakel is born in Leeuwarden to a Reformed pastor of extraordinary piety.

1659   Brakel studies theology at Utrecht under Gisbertus Voetius and others.

1662   After receiving theological training, Brakel begins ministering in the
        national church of the Netherlands, where he would serve five churches
        over the course of nearly fifty years.

1676   Voetius dies on November 1.

1707   The third, expanded, and definitive edition of Brakel's *The Christian's
        Reasonable Service* is published.

1711   Having become very ill, Brakel dies on October 30.

Did You Know?

- Voetius was married to his wife, Deliana, for sixty-four years and they had ten children, two of whom became professors at Utrecht like their father.

- As a polemical theologian, Voetius's strong positions and attacks of opposing views often isolated him. Loneliness assailed him at times but he viewed it as part of the price he was called to pay for taking a stand for biblical, Reformed truth.

- On his deathbed, a visitor asked Brakel how his soul was faring. "Very well," was his response. "I may rest in my Jesus; I am united to Him and I am awaiting His coming for me."

- For family worship, a typical eighteenth-century Dutch farmer would read a "stukje van Vader Brakel" [a piece or selection from Father Brakel] every night to his family after the reading of Scripture.

Their Legacy

There are three key lessons that we can learn from the pastors and theologians of the *Nadere Reformatie*.

Continuing Reformation

As the name of the movement indicates, the Dutch Further Reformation was an attempt to further the initial Reformation in the Netherlands. It was governed by a sense that reform needed to penetrate more intimately into personal lives, the church's worship, and society as a whole. The motto was, "the Reformed church needs to be ever reforming." But as Herman Witsius stressed, this continuing reform applies only to the church's life and not to doctrine, since Reformation doctrine was already established as foundational truth. What the *Nadere Reformatie* was seeking, according to Heinrich Heppe, was "the completion of the church reformation of the sixteenth century (as being a mere reform of doctrine) by way of a revival of piety or by a reformation of life." Their motto ought to be the motto of every church and every Christian—always and ever reforming.

Experiential, Practical Theology

The father of the *Nadere Reformatie,* Willem Teellinck, said, "The true Christian faith is knowledge that leads to godliness." Voetius, responding to the objection that Reformed theologians disregard practice in favor of theoretical knowledge, wrote, "The very light of the facts is enough to destroy this calumny, since the sermons of the most distinguished of our preachers and an almost infinite number of writings of the Reformers breathe pure practice, so that our theologians, like Socrates, may be said to have brought theology from heaven down to earth, or, better, to have raised it to heaven from the earth and scholastic dust." These men stressed that all theology must be practical, being used to encourage the spiritual exercise of divine graces. Brakel prayed in the preface of his great theological work: "May it be to the conversion of the unconverted, the instruction of the ignorant, the restoration of backsliders, the encouragement of the discouraged, as well as to the growth of faith, hope, and love in all who have become partakers of a measure of grace."

God-Honoring Academia

Voetius, serving as a theological professor for over forty years, believed his duty at Utrecht was to "practically treat of the solid and orthodox science of theology, which is by its nature practical." All his scholasticism, as well as that promoted by the other Dutch Further Reformation divines, had the edification of the church as its ultimate goal. In 1664, Voetius published "The Exercises and Library of a Studious Theologian," a comprehensive 700-page introduction to theological literature and a four-year program of theological study. Its theme is one with his overall vision: theology must be known and practiced. While stressing the importance and necessity of sound theological education, this movement militated against "ivory tower" theologians.

Reflect

1. In order for a life to be continually reformed by God's Word, there must be a need for ongoing reformation. What are some areas in your thinking and living that are in need of reform? Are there areas in your life that contradict the doctrine you claim to believe?

2. The *Nadere Reformatie* stressed that an ever-expanding knowledge of the truth of Scripture is essential to a life of godliness. How could you more effectively and strategically seek to grow in theological knowledge?

3. When you hear the terms "scholasticism" and "academia," do primarily negative thoughts come into your mind? Why, or why not?

Discuss

1. It is common in our day to hear people say, "Don't give me theology. I want something practical." How would you respond to this? What is the fundamental fallacy of this assertion?

2. What does it mean to "practice" theology? What are the practical implications of a doctrine like the providence of God or the threefold office of Christ?

3. Why can true theology never be merely an intellectual theory? And why can true piety never be void of knowledge of the truth?

4. Both Voetius and Brakel were involved in various religious and theological controversies in their day. How did their understanding of the relationship between right doctrine and right living fuel their passion for defending the truth against error?

Read

Primary Sources

à Brakel, Wilhelmus. *The Christian's Reasonable Service.* 4 volumes. Translated by Bartel Elshout. Edited by Joel R. Beeke. Grand Rapids: Reformation Heritage Books, 1995. (For an introduction on the *Nadere Reformatie,* see 1: lxxxv-cxi.)

Saldenus, Guilelmus, and Wilhelmus à Brakel. *In Remembrance of Him: Profiting from the Lord's Supper.* Translated by Bartel Elshout. Edited by James A. DeJong. Grand Rapids: Reformation Heritage Books, 2012.

Voetius, Gisbertus, and Johannes Hoornbeeck. *Spiritual Desertion.* Translated by John Vriend and Harry Boonstra. Edited by M. Eugene Osterhaven. Grand Rapids: Reformation Heritage Books, 2009.

Secondary Sources

Beeke, Joel R. *Gisbertus Voetius: Toward a Reformed Marriage of Knowledge and Piety.* Grand Rapids: Reformation Heritage Books, 1999.

Elshout, Bartel. *The Pastoral and Practical Theology of Wilhelmus à Brakel.* Grand Rapids: Reformation Heritage Books, 1997.

Scottish "Puritan":
Samuel Rutherford

Lesson Given by Ian Hamilton

Meditate

Rutherford once said, "Next to Christ I had but one joy—to preach Christ my Lord." Meditate on Ephesians 3:8.

Learn

Ian Hamilton states, "By common consent Samuel Rutherford was one of the greatest ministers of the Scottish church." Though not from England, this Presbyterian divine was united to the English Puritans by the closest spiritual bonds of doctrine, worship, and church order.

His Life

1600   Rutherford is born in Nisbet, Roxburghshire, to a well-to-do farmer.

1617   He begins his studies at the University of Edinburgh, graduating with his master of arts degree four years later.

1620   Rutherford is most likely brought to saving faith in Christ during this year.

1623   He is installed as Professor of Humanity at Edinburgh.

1626   Rutherford is forced to resign due to accusations of fornication with the woman he will end up marrying.

1627   He is called to pastor the church in Anwoth by the Solway, a rural parish.

1636   Due to his publication of an anti-Arminian work, Rutherford is summoned before the High Court for a trial which ends in his exile to Aberdeen.

1638   After the National Covenant was signed, he returns to Anwoth.

1639   Rutherford is appointed Professor of Theology at St. Mary's College, St. Andrews.

1643   He is called to be one of six Scottish Commissioners to the Westminster Assembly.

1647   Rutherford returns from the Westminster Assembly to St. Mary's College, where he will teach and preach until the year of his death.

1661   Having been charged with treason and deprived of his positions within the church and university, Rutherford dies.

Did You Know?

- Rutherford was known to rise at 3 a.m. in order to devote himself to hours of prayer and meditation upon the Word.

- During his exile in Aberdeen, Rutherford wrote to his congregation in Anwoth, expressing how Christ had sanctified his trial: "I never knew, by mine nine years' preaching, so much of Christ's love, as He has taught me in Aberdeen."

- On his death bed, Rutherford exhorted his fellow ministers, saying, "Dear brethren, do all for Christ. Pray for Christ. Preach for Christ. Beware of men-pleasing." He had reckoned with the apostle's words in Galatians 1:10.

- C. H. Spurgeon said that Rutherford's *Letters* were "the nearest thing to inspiration which can be found in all the writings of mere men." Is that not a good incentive to read them?

His Legacy

Hamilton presents three reasons why Christians throughout the centuries have been attracted to Rutherford's *Letters*. He says, "They are drawn to the Christocentrism of the letters. They are drawn to the heavenly-mindedness of the letters. They are drawn to the way Rutherford can write about suffering in ways that warm and energize the Christian heart." These three points get to the marrow of Rutherford's thought.

Infatuated with Christ

Rutherford's thinking was pervaded with a warm and intense love for Christ. He writes, "There is none like Him; I would not exchange one smile of His lovely face with kingdoms…. let others take their silly, feckless heaven in this life. Envy them not; but let your soul…cast at all things and disdain them, except one only: either Christ or nothing." Rutherford had found the One who alone was worthy of his heart's affections. He would gladly give up all, even heaven itself, to have his Lord: "I know not a thing worth the buying but heaven; and my own mind is, if comparison were made betwixt Christ and heaven, I would sell heaven with my blessing, and buy Christ." This all-consuming infatuation with Christ is the key to understanding Rutherford.

Fixed on Eternity

The intensity of his love for Christ made Rutherford long for eternity. He vents his longing for heaven, "Oh, how long is it to the dawning of the marriage day! O sweet Jesus, take wide steps! O my Lord, come over the mountain at one stride." This earnestness of desire for the glory to come enabled him to be of much earthly use in the hands of his Master. It freed him from holding to the things of this world too tightly, and thereby fit him for sacrificial service in Christ's cause.

Acquainted with Sorrow

Rutherford was no stranger to grief, loss, and suffering. But in it all he saw the loving purpose of his God. He questions, "Why should I tremble at the plough of my Lord that maketh deep furrows on my soul? I know He is no idle husbandman; He purposeth a crop." Rutherford knew that every earthly sorrow the Lord brought upon him was but a means of conforming him to Christ and fitting him for glory. "Oh what owe I," he exclaimed, "to the file, to the hammer, to the furnace of my Lord Jesus!"

Reflect

1. How does the love and fervor of Rutherford's pursuit of Christ challenge you? Do you resonate with his statements about the loveliness of Christ?

2. Rutherford passionately gave his life for the kirk (church) of Scotland though he believed her to be "a harlot." He refused to abandon her, but labored to see her reformed according to God's Word. How can you be humbly striving for reform in your local congregation?

3. Rutherford spoke of his indebtedness to Christ's file, hammer, and furnace. Do you respond to suffering with such gratitude and trust in God's good purpose?

Discuss

1. Hamilton describes Rutherford as "a flawed Christian" who was greatly used by God. How does this encourage you? How does this magnify the glory and power of God (1 Cor. 1:26–31)?

2. What do we learn from Rutherford's enmity toward his fellow Christians who were in the Resolutioner camp? How are Christians to foster peace even in the face of significant disagreements? What is the relationship between unity and truth?

3. Rutherford was quoted in the lesson as saying, "Grace withereth without adversity." What does this mean? How does this transform the way you view your sufferings?

4. Rutherford's last words were, "Immanuel's land, Immanuel's land. I will go erelong to that high land which is Immanuel's land." What does this say about his assurance of salvation? What can we learn about dying well from Rutherford?

Read

Primary Sources

Rutherford, Samuel. *Communion Sermons*. Dallas: Blue Banner, 1986.

Rutherford, Samuel. *The Letters of Samuel Rutherford*. Edinburgh: Banner of Truth Trust, 1984.

Rutherford, Samuel. *Quaint Sermons of Samuel Rutherford*. Morgan, PA: Soli Deo Gloria, 1999.

Rutherford, Samuel. *The Trial and Triumph of Faith*. Edinburgh: Banner of Truth Trust, 2001.

Secondary Sources

Barnes, Stanley. *An Inspirational Treasury of Samuel Rutherford*. Belfast: Ambassador, 2001.

Rendell, Kingsley. Samuel Rutherford: *A New Biography of the Man & His Ministry*. Fearn, UK: Christian Focus, 2003.

Twentieth-Century "Puritan":
D. Martyn Lloyd-Jones

Lesson Given by Jason Meyer

Meditate

Lloyd-Jones once preached, "Do not tell me about your good works, I am not interested. Do not tell me you are a church member, I am not a bit interested. Are you glorying in the cross? Is this everything to you? Is this life to you? Are you ready to die rather than deny this glorious message?" Meditate on Galatians 6:14.

Learn

The Scottish minister Eric Alexander wrote, "There is little doubt that Dr. Martyn Lloyd-Jones was the greatest preacher the English-speaking world has seen in the twentieth century." John MacArthur went further to say, "When the final chapter of church history is written, I believe the Doctor will stand as one of the greatest preachers of all time."

His Life

1899   Lloyd-Jones is born in Cardiff, Wales, to Henry and Magdalen.

1923   He earns a doctorate of medicine from London University and grows in prominence as a physician.

1923   Lloyd-Jones, who prior had been very religious, undergoes a true conversion to Christ through the preaching of John Hutton at Westminster Chapel.

1926   With much inner turmoil, he leaves the medical world to become a preacher.

1927   After marrying Bethan Phillips, Lloyd-Jones becomes the pastor of a small congregation in Aberavon, being ordained as a Calvinistic Methodist.

1939   Lloyd-Jones accepts the invitation from G. Campbell Morgan to be the associate pastor at Westminster Chapel, London.

1943   Morgan retires, leaving Lloyd-Jones as the sole pastor of the Chapel.

1954   Lloyd-Jones hosts the inaugural Puritan Conference at Westminster Chapel.

1957   He supports the establishment of the Banner of Truth Trust, which would reprint many of the classic Puritan works then unavailable.

1968   Lloyd-Jones, due to colon cancer, retires from his ministry at Westminster Chapel, spending the rest of his days writing and preaching around the world.

1981   He dies in his sleep at Ealing on March 1.

Did You Know?

- When Lloyd-Jones gave up his medical career to become a minister, his salary went from 3,500 pounds to 225 pounds a year. In response, he said, "I gave up nothing, I received everything. I count it the highest honor that God can confer on any man to call him to be a herald of the gospel."

- In 1927 when Lloyd-Jones first began his pastorate, he had received no formal training and had preached less than a dozen times.

- Lloyd-Jones's weekly preaching typically followed this pattern: an experiential message for believers on Sunday morning, an evangelistic message for unbelievers on Sunday evening, and a doctrinal message on Friday evening.

- The simple tombstone of Lloyd-Jones records the words preached in his first sermon: "For I determined not to know anything among you save Jesus Christ and Him crucified."

His Legacy

Lloyd-Jones commented that ever since reading a biography on Richard Baxter in 1925 "a true and living interest in the Puritans and their works has gripped me, and I am free to confess that my whole ministry has been governed by this." Though technically not a Puritan in the historical sense of the term, Lloyd-Jones was profoundly influenced by Puritanism and sought to spread it far and wide in the twentieth century.

Experiential, Soul-Searching Preaching

In his famous lectures on preaching given at Westminster Theological Seminary, Lloyd-Jones encouraged his hearers to read the Puritans. He said, "Those men were preachers, they were practical, experimental preachers.... As you read them you will find that they not only give you knowledge and information, they at the same time do something to you." Lloyd-Jones himself had been powerfully worked upon through his reading of Puritan sermons and books. From them he learned how to apply the Scriptures experientially to the souls of his hearers, not merely informing their minds but affecting their hearts.

Purity in Christ's Church

Lloyd-Jones concluded his lecture "The Puritans and Their Origins" by stating, "The Puritan is primarily concerned about a pure church, a truly Reformed Church." By this he meant that Puritanism largely aimed to reform not only the church's doctrine but also her practice. Puritan ministers stressed the corporateness of the church over individualism, the authority of Scripture over tradition, the simplicity and spirituality of worship over the ornate and external worship of Rome, and the faithful and diligent administration of church discipline. Lloyd-Jones powerfully remarked, "If we fail to put the doctrine of the church in a central position we are departing from the true Puritan attitude, the Puritan outlook, the Puritan spirit, and the Puritan understanding."

Christ-Exalting Revival

The reason he encouraged the reading of the Puritans, said Lloyd-Jones, was so that "we may be crushed to our knees with a sense of humility and be made to cry to God that He would visit us again." He was convinced that the reading of these men would bring us face-to-face with our low spiritual condition, causing us to cry out to God for fresh outpourings of His Spirit. He elsewhere explained that "revival, above everything else, is a glorification of the Lord Jesus Christ, the Son of God. It is the restoration of him to the center of the life of the Church. You find this warm devotion, personal devotion, to him." By reading the Christ-saturated Puritans, Christians, under the Spirit's blessing, would be stirred up in the pursuit of such whole-souled devotion to Jesus on both an individual and a corporate level.

Reflect

1. Lloyd-Jones, clearly living for another world, gave up the prospect of fame and fortune as a physician to preach in an obscure, poverty-stricken church. Which world are you living for?

2. Jason Meyer, recounting the fearlessness of Lloyd-Jones when a bomb fell near the Chapel, says that he had "doctrinal steel" in his soul. Have the doctrines of Scripture so fortified and strengthened your soul? Or do you find yourself blown about by every wind and wave of life? How can you cultivate such heartiness of soul?

3. Lloyd-Jones wrote, "However much a man may admire aspects of Puritanism, if his first concern is not for a pure church...he surely has no right to call himself a Puritan." What does a pure church look like? How important to you is the purity of the church?

Discuss

1. Meyer states that Lloyd-Jones found a "living Calvinism" in the Puritans that incorporated both the objective and the subjective aspects of biblical Christianity. What is meant by this? What is the result of the objective being stressed to the neglect of the subjective, or vice versa?

2. In God's providence, Lloyd-Jones was trained as a medical physician, not a preacher or theologian. How did his experience as a doctor equip him to be a suitable physician of the souls of men?

3. Lloyd-Jones defines the Puritans as "experimental preachers." What is meant by *experimental*? How does this term differ from *practical*?

4. In an age where revival was particularly man-centered, Lloyd-Jones's assertion that revival is essentially about the exaltation of Christ was unheard of. Does this challenge your understanding of revival? How are we to pursue this "restoration of [Christ] to the center of the life of the church" today?

Read

Primary Sources

Lloyd-Jones, D. M. *Experiencing the New Birth: Studies in John 3*. Wheaton, IL: Crossway, 2015.

Lloyd-Jones, D. M. *The Puritans: Their Origins and Successors*. Edinburgh: Banner of Truth Trust, 1987.

Lloyd-Jones, D. M. *Spiritual Depression: Its Causes and Cure*. Grand Rapids: Eerdmans, 1998.

Secondary Sources

Catherwood, Christopher. *From Wales to Westminster: The Story of Dr. Martyn Lloyd-Jones*. Fearn, UK: Christian Focus, 1999.

Murray, Iain. The Life of D. *Martyn Lloyd-Jones, 1899–1981*. Edinburgh: Banner of Truth Trust, 2014.

PART THREE

Puritan Teaching

The Westminster Assembly

Lesson Given by Chad Van Dixhoorn

Meditate

B. B. Warfield, discussing the first question of the Westminster Shorter Catechism, wrote, "According to the Reformed conception man exists not merely that God may be glorified in him, but that he may delight in this glorious God. It does justice to the subjective as well as to the objective side of the case.... No man is truly Reformed in his thought, then, unless he conceives of man not merely as destined to be the instrument of the Divine glory, but also as destined to reflect the glory of God in his own consciousness, to exult in God: nay, unless he himself delights in God as the all-glorious One." Meditate on Psalm 73:25–26.

Learn

Richard Baxter wrote of the Westminster Assembly, "The divines there congregated were men of eminent learning and godliness and ministerial abilities and fidelity; and, being not worthy to be one of them myself, I may the more freely speak that truth which I know, even in the face of malice and envy, that as far as I am able to judge by the information of all history of that kind, and by any other evidence left us, the Christian world since the days of the apostles had never a synod of more excellent divines...than this Synod and the Synod of Dort."

Key Dates

The Westminster Assembly held around 1,400 sessions over a span of ten years. Below are some of the key dates of what Chad Van Dixhoorn called "the high point of the Puritan experiment."

1643   The Assembly is called by Parliament and begins to meet on July 1.

1644   In December, the Form of Church Government is submitted to Parliament.

1645   The Directory for Public Worship is completed and approved by Parliament.

1646   The Confession of Faith is presented to the House of Commons, with Scriptures being added the following year.

1647   The Larger and Shorter Catechisms are completed, being sent to Parliament with proof texts in April of the following year.

1649   After the execution of Charles I, the last numbered session of the Assembly is recorded on February 22.

1653   The Assembly dissolves, no longer operating as a committee for examining ministers.

Key Documents

While around 140 documents were produced during the Westminster Assembly, the most significant ones will be introduced here.

The Confession of Faith

Sinclair Ferguson writes, "The Westminster Confession of Faith is one of the noblest and most influential documents of the Christian Church. It remains the fullest and most carefully constructed brief exposition of the Christian faith ever written." This 33-chapter document, intended to replace the 39 Articles of the Church of England, sets forth a concise, systematic summary of biblical truth. Beginning with the doctrine of Scripture and ending with eschatological judgment, the Westminster Confession built upon centuries of creedal formulation and the best of Reformation exegesis and theology, comprising what Van Dixhoorn says is perhaps "the wisest of creeds in its teaching and the finest in its doctrinal expression." The Confession, under God's blessing, has had a monumental impact on the church up to the present day.

The Catechisms

The Shorter Catechism consists of 107 questions with concise, sentence-long answers intended for memorization. The Larger Catechism has a total of 196 questions with more extended and complex answers, being designed as a teaching aid for Christians. The answers provided by the divines evidence their profound grasp of Scripture. For example, early on the Assembly met to formulate an answer to the question, "What is God?" They decided that its youngest member, most likely George Gillespie, should attempt an answer. Sensing his utter insufficiency to articulate the essence of the divine Being, however, he suggested that they look to God for help. He then prayed, "O God, thou art a spirit, infinite, eternal, and unchangeable, in thy being, wisdom, power, holiness, justice, goodness, and truth." This was quickly recorded by another member of the Assembly and was adopted as the best conceivable answer! Along with its concise statements of biblical doctrine, the Catechisms also give careful and lengthy attention to biblical ethics, providing thorough expositions of the Ten Commandments.

The Directory for Public Worship

The men gathered at Westminster Abbey were jealous for the purity of God's worship and sought to reform the corruptions which they perceived in the Church of England. One of the Scottish Commissioners to the Assembly spoke of the "superstition and idolatry in worship...which we hope, through the blessing of God upon this work, shall be brought to an end." Seeking to replace the Book of Common Prayer, the Directory of Public Worship set out to provide broad guidelines for church worship, not an authoritative liturgy. In 14 dense chapters, it sets forth a miniature pastoral theology, providing scriptural wisdom on matters such as preaching, public prayer, the administration of the sacraments, officiating weddings, and even visiting the sick. John Murray writes, "In the Directory for Public Worship, we have one of the finest fruits of the work of the Assembly.... Nothing in human literature will afford us better instruction in the dignity and decorum that ought to characterize the public worship of God." The church today would do well to study and heed the wisdom of this great work on God's worship.

Reflect

1. Question 1 of the Shorter Catechism asks, "What is the chief end of man?" The Answer: "Man's chief end is to glorify God, and to enjoy him forever." Do you enjoy and delight in God? What is the relationship between glorifying God and enjoying Him?

2. Why did the Westminster divines devote so much time to expounding the Ten Commandments? How central is the law of God in your own life?

3. Have you ever memorized the Westminster Shorter Catechism? If not, why not start now? How could the knowledge of such truth strengthen you in your Christian walk and witness?

Discuss

1. What is the relationship of creeds and confessions to the Scripture? What kind of authority ought creedal statements to wield in the life of the church?

2. Why are creeds and confessions necessary? How would you respond to someone who argues that Christians ought to have no creed but the Bible?

3. Why would the Assembly take the time to draw up two catechisms after already having written up a confession of faith? Wouldn't the Confession have been sufficient to teach biblical doctrine?

4. The Westminster Confession begins with chapters on the doctrine of Scripture and God. Why did the divines begin here? What does this teach us about the nature of true theology?

Read

_____

Primary Sources

Beeke, Joel and Sinclair Ferguson, eds. *Reformed Confessions Harmonized.*
Grand Rapids: Baker, 1999.

Van Dixhoorn, Chad, ed. *The Minutes and Papers of the Westminster Assembly.*
5 volumes. Oxford: Oxford University Press, 2012.

Secondary Sources

Van Dixhoorn, Chad. *Confessing the Faith: A Reader's Guide to the Westminster Confession of Faith.* Edinburgh: Banner of Truth Trust, 2014.

Whyte, Alexander. *An Exposition on the Shorter Catechism.* Fearn, UK:
Christian Focus, 2001.

Vos, Johannes. *The Westminster Larger Catechism: A Commentary.* Philipsburg, NJ:
Presbyterian & Reformed, 2002.

Letham, Robert. *The Westminster Assembly: Reading Its Theology in Historical Context.* Philipsburg, NJ: Presbyterian & Reformed, 2009.

Puritans on Regeneration and Conversion

Lesson Given by John Snyder

Meditate

Richard Sibbes wrote, "As the minister speaks to the ear, Christ speaks, opens, and unlocks the heart at the same time; and gives it power to open, not from itself, but from Christ.... The manner of working of the reasonable creature, is to work freely by a sweet inclination, not by violence. Therefore when he works the work of conversion, he doth it in a sweet manner, though it be mighty for the efficaciousness of it." Meditate on 2 Corinthians 4:6.

Learn

Regeneration

The Puritans, standing against the externalism and ritualism of the Church of England, stressed the necessity of the new birth. Thomas Watson counters the idea that one is saved by the baptismal waters, stating, "It is not baptism which makes a Christian; many are no better than baptized heathens. The essential part of religion lies in the new creature." Neither is one a Christian merely by possessing doctrinal knowledge. As Stephen Charnock cautions, "An evangelical head will be but drier fuel for eternal burning, without an evangelical impression upon the heart and the badge of a new nature." One must be born again if he is to enter into the kingdom of heaven (John 3:3–5).

The Sinner's Necessity

Fallen man, being spiritually dead in sin, is both unwilling and unable to come to Christ. The Westminster Confession states that by the corruption conveyed through Adam, "we are utterly indisposed, disabled, and made opposite to all good, and wholly inclined to all evil." Man is unable to come to Christ because he is unwilling to come to Christ, and he is unwilling to come to Christ because he hates Christ. For, as Thomas Hooker wrote, sin has taken the human heart captive so that "corruption exerciseth a sovereign power and command over the will." If ever he is to respond in faith to the gospel, he must first be quickened by God Himself.

The Spirit's Agency

The Puritans stressed that regeneration is a sovereign working of God's Spirit. Since it involves a new heart and a new spirit, the natural man, being spiritually dead, cannot produce this new birth in himself. The believer can concur with the Spirit in his sanctification, said John Flavel, "but in the first production of this spiritual principle he can do nothing." It is the Spirit, wrote George Swinnock, who is the "efficient principle of it." The Spirit, being the bond between believers and Christ, makes sinners alive in the Savior. In this way, affirms Thomas Cole, "Regeneration is the Implantation of the Soul into Christ."

The Scripture's Instrumentality

Though the Puritans were quite clear in maintaining the truth that God alone is the primary cause of regeneration, they also maintained that God ordinarily used the Bible as His instrument. William Whately wrote, "The Spirit of God, that could work of himself, and without means, pleaseth not so to do in this great work: but of his own free-will makes choice for himself, of a fit and blessed instrument for that purpose; even the law of God, the whole doctrine of the Scriptures." John Brinsley wrote that God draws men to Christ by the Word, "sweetly overpowering their wills, making them willing to come unto him."

Conversion

The result of God's regenerating work is the soul's conversion to God. Stephen Charnock explains, "Regeneration is a spiritual change, conversion is a spiritual motion.... Conversion is related to regeneration, as the effect to the cause. Life precedes motion, and is the cause of motion...as a child in its first formation in the womb, contributes nothing to the first infusion of life; but after it hath life, it is active." True conversion is manifested in faith, repentance, and new obedience.

Faith

The Spirit does not force us to believe in Christ against our wills; He transforms our minds and wills so that we can do nothing other than come to Christ for salvation and life. This is why the immediate and necessary response of the regenerate soul is a Christ-directed faith. Perkins defines saving faith as "a miraculous and supernatural faculty of the heart, apprehending Christ Jesus being applied by the operation of the holy Ghost, and receiving him to itself." Such a faith lays hold of Christ and rests upon Him alone for total salvation. A living faith, said David Clarkson, makes men "sensible of their misery by reason of sin and wrath...convinced of an absolute necessity of Christ," so that they think, "Give us Christ, or else we die."

Repentance

Saving faith is always a repentant faith. "To repent," wrote Clarkson, "is to turn from sin...and involves a turning to God. In this turning there are three steps: sorrow for sin, hatred of sin, and a resolve to forsake sin." The Puritans heralded the biblical teaching that true conversion to God entails not only an embracing of Christ, but a forsaking of sin. Again Clarkson warns, "Many will not part with that which keeps them at a distance from Christ. They will not part with sin to come to Christ, and there is no coming to him without turning from that."

Obedience

A converted life, exercising faith and repentance, is one of conformity to God's revealed will. Speaking of God's regenerating work, Jonathan Edwards said, "As it reaches the bottom of the heart, and changes the nature, so it will effectually dispose to a universal obedience. It shows God as worthy to be obeyed and served. It draws forth the heart in a sincere love of God...and it convinces of the reality of those glorious rewards that God has promised to them that obey him." The Puritans did not believe that one who was the recipient of regenerating grace and who had turned from sin to God could continue in a habitual lifestyle of lawlessness. The Spirit, in transforming the heart, writes the law of God upon it and inclines it to live for God.

Reflect

1. The Puritan understanding of regeneration flowed not only from their affirmation of God's sovereignty in salvation but also from their affirmation of the radical corruption of man in sin. Do you agree that because of man's deadness and enslavement in sin, he cannot and will not come to God? How does this increase your gratitude for your salvation?

2. Does your life evidence the faith, repentance, and obedience which mark true conversion?

3. Are you continuing to grow as a new man or woman in Christ, possessing an ever-deepening faith and repentance, as well as an increasing zeal for holiness?

Discuss

1. John Snyder states, "The Puritans were never interested in a merely theoretical theology." What was the reason for their disinterest? Why must Christianity never be a mere theory but instead experienced and practiced?

2. How are all three Persons of the Trinity involved in our regeneration?

3. What is the relationship between faith and repentance? Does one cause the other?

4. The Puritans stressed that an utterly lawless life is an unconverted life. Why can't a Christian continue in sin that grace may abound (Rom. 6:1ff.)?

Read

___

Primary Sources

Charnock, Stephen. "The Necessity of Regeneration" and "A Discourse of the Nature of Regeneration." In *The Complete Works of Stephen Charnock,* 7–165. Edinburgh: Banner of Truth Trust, 1985.

Hopkins, Ezekiel. *The Nature and Necessity of Regeneration; Or, the New Birth.* In *The Works of Ezekiel Hopkins,* 2:221–98. Morgan, PA: Soli Deo Gloria, 1997.

Watson, Thomas. *The Doctrine of Repentance.* Edinburgh: Banner of Truth Trust, 1988.

Secondary Sources

Beeke, Joel and Mark Jones. "The Puritans on Regeneration." In *A Puritan Theology: Doctrine for Life,* 463–80. Grand Rapids: Reformation Heritage Books, 2012.

Kistler, Don. *The Puritans on Conversion.* Morgan, PA: Soli Deo Gloria, 1990.

Puritans on Conscience

Lesson Given by David Murray

Meditate

Joseph Hall wrote, "Happy is that man, that can be acquitted by himself in private, by others in public, and by God in both." Meditate on Acts 24:16.

Learn

Conscience was a tremendous and inescapable reality to the Puritans. They believed it to be a universal faculty of human nature by which God established His authority in the soul for men to judge themselves rationally. And they believed it was central to a life of godliness. Thus, they developed what became known as *casuistry*, or what would today be called *biblical counseling*. Through the application of Scripture, they sought to awaken and shape the consciences of their people for the glory of God.

Principles of Puritan Casuistry

Puritan counseling of the conscience possessed a number of fundamental characteristics which enabled it to be maximally effective.

Biblical

The Puritans believed that the great means of counseling were the application of the Word of Christ and prayer to the Father, both done in the Holy Spirit. William Perkins wrote, "All actions that please God, must be done in faith; therefore all actions that please God, must have some ground and direction in the word of God, without which word of God there can be no faith." Richard Sibbes stated that Christians "have the book of God to rectify the inward book of conscience." The Word of God is given to us to instruct our consciences, and consciences are given to us so that we may live in subjection to God's Word.

Holistic

Possessing a robustly biblical anthropology that acknowledged the complexity of human nature and its condition in sin, Puritan divines sought to address each counseling situation in a comprehensive fashion. Baxter, in his thorough treatment of depression, notes, "With very many there is a great part of the cause in distemper, weakness, and diseasedness of the body; and by it the soul is greatly disabled to any comfortable sense. But the more it ariseth from such natural necessity, the less sinful and less dangerous to the soul; but never the less troublesome, but the more." The Puritans reckoned with the role of physical, temperamental, spiritual, and demonic causes when dealing with wounded and struggling souls.

Christ-Centered

John Owen said, "It is by a principle of Gospel light alone that conscience is directed to condemn all sin, and yet to acquit all sinners that are purged." Sibbes added that through Christ's "superabundant obedience" alone can one's conscience find true peace and calm. Not only, however, is the conscience cleansed in Christ, but the Christian is renewed and enabled to walk in obedience to God, preventing his conscience from being marred by sin. In this way, a good conscience is based upon Christ's finished work, and is guarded by our obedience through Christ.

Practice of Puritan Casuistry

The principles of casuistry would be useless if they were not put into practice. The Puritans were master physicians of the soul who not only knew how to minister the Word to consciences, but also sought to train their people to do the same.

Practical Syllogism

David Dickson defined conscience as "the understanding power of our souls examining how matters do stand betwixt God and us, comparing his will revealed, with our state, condition and carriage, in thoughts, words or deeds, done or omitted, and passing judgment thereupon as the case requires." The Puritans believed that the conscience carries out its God-given task by way of syllogistic argumentation. This form of reasoning includes a major premise stating a general principle, then a minor premise stating an observation or fact, then a conclusion that results from putting these premises together. William Ames illustrates how the conscience so reasons in both regenerate and unregenerate. The conscience may condemn, saying, "He that lives in sin, shall die: I live in sin; Therefore, I shall die." But the conscience may also proclaim gospel comfort: "Whosoever believes in Christ, shall not die but live. I believe in Christ; Therefore, I shall not die but live."

Pointed Application

According to the Puritans, the pastor needed skill in dealing with various cases of conscience, applying the Word both from the pulpit and in one-on-one counseling sessions. William Ames wrote, "Because of this slowness in men to conclude, and apply, there is necessity laid on all Ministers, not only to declare God's will generally; but likewise so far as they are able, to help, and further, both publicly and in private, the application of it, so far as men's condition and consciences require." Because of the various types of evil consciences which can deceive Christian and non-Christian alike, a herald of God's truth is often needed as the means to wake up and reform its errors.

Persistent Maintenance

Drawing from passages like Acts 24:16, Romans 2:15, and Hebrews 9:14, the Puritans believed it to be the duty of all Christians to maintain a good conscience. Sibbes exhorted, "Let us every day keep an audit within doors, every day cast up our accounts, every day draw the blood of Christ over our accounts, every day beg forgiveness of sins, and the Spirit of Christ to lead us, that so we may keep account every day, that we may make our reckonings every day.... This should be the daily practice of a Christian, and then he may lay himself down in peace."

Reflect

1. How central do you consider conscience to be to your spiritual health? Are you actively seeking to maintain a good conscience before God and man?

2. Is there known sin in your life which is unconfessed? What are the dangers of failing to bring your defiled conscience to Christ (cf. 1 Tim. 1:19)?

3. Is there any area of life where you are willfully disobeying God's law? Or any truth of God's Word that you are unwilling to submit unto? If so, what does this reveal about your conscience?

Discuss

1. Why was the conscience so central in Puritan theology? Did they overemphasize this faculty of the soul?

2. Richard Sibbes said, "Conscience is either the greatest friend or the greatest enemy in the world." Why is this? How is the conscience a most helpful companion to the Christian through this earthly pilgrimage?

3. What were some of the types of evil consciences mentioned by David Murray? How ought the Scriptures to be applied to each in particular?

4. Acts 24:16 speaks about the relation of our consciences toward both God and our fellow man. How does our conscience relate to our neighbor? What does it mean to keep a good conscience before men?

Read

Primary Sources

Watson, Thomas. *Precious Remedies against Satan's Devices.* Edinburgh: Banner of Truth Trust, 1968.

Bridge, William. *A Lifting Up of the Downcast.* Edinburgh: Banner of Truth Trust, 1961.

Bolton, Robert. *General Directions for a Comfortable Walking with God.* Morgan, PA: Soli Deo Gloria, 1997.

Secondary Sources

Beeke, Joel and Mark Jones. "The Puritans on Conscience" and "Puritan Casuistry." In *A Puritan Theology: Doctrine for Life,* 909–45. Grand Rapids: Reformation Heritage Books, 2012.

Deckard, Mark. *Helpful Truth in Past Places: The Puritan Practice of Biblical Counseling.* Fearn, UK: Christian Focus, 2009.

Packer, J. I. "The Puritan Conscience." In *Puritan Papers, Volume 2, 1960–1962,* 237–57. Phillipsburg, NJ: Presbyterian & Reformed, 2001.

Puritans on Zeal

Lesson Given by James La Belle

Meditate

Samuel Ward wrote, "Zeal is as strong as death, hot as the coals of juniper, floods of many waters cannot quench it. Agar [Prov. 30:29–31] speaks of four things, stately in their kind; I will make bold to add a fifth, comprehending and exceeding them all, namely the zealous Christian; [he is as] strong and bold as the lion, not turning his head for any; as swift as the greyhound in the ways of God's commandments, in the race to heaven; as nimble as the goat, climbing the steep and craggy mountains of piety and virtue; [and as] a victorious king, overcoming the world and his lusts; Solomon in all his royalty is not clothed like [a zealous Christian] in his fiery chariot." Meditate on Romans 12:11.

Learn

James La Belle addresses a topic little spoken of in the church of Christ today, but one which the Scriptures and the Puritans speak much of—sacred zeal.

The Nature of Zeal

La Belle helpfully defines Christian zeal as "a sacred flame lit by God in the soul, which sets all the affections on fire for God and results in all of life being lived for His glory." In a similar fashion, Oliver Bowles described zeal as "a holy ardor kindled by the Holy Spirit of God in the affections, improving a man to the utmost for God's glory, and the Church's good.... It is not so much any one affection, as the intended degree of all." By nature, Christian zeal is the grace that invigorates and inflames all our affections toward a sole purpose and, more specifically, a holy purpose. It is the divine grace that enables the once barren affections to bring forth the fruits of righteousness in every area of life.

The Marks of Zeal

Such sacred zeal has defining characteristics which distinguish it from false religious zeal. First, it is marked by love for God. John Reynolds said, "It pleads the beauties of His face, the pleasures of His presence, and cries out, 'When shall I appear before God in Zion?'" This zeal creates a hunger and thirst for God, and an impatient desire to be with Him. Second, it is ruled by Scripture. John Evans asserted, "Indeed heat without light, or rash and blind zeal, is the most extravagant and mischievous thing in the world." If we are to honor and serve God, whom we fervently love, we must know what His will and good pleasure are. That requires us to have constant regard for His Word. Third, it is devoted to good works. One zealous Christian, said Ward, "is worth a thousand others, one doth the work of many." Such a man will summon all the powers of soul and body to accomplish the work the Lord has given him. Finally, it cares deeply about others, especially their eternal welfare. William Beveridge wrote, "If we have any zeal for [God's] glory, it will appear in striving all we can to spread and propagate His said Gospel.... All who are truly zealous for His honor, cannot but be so likewise for the salvation of all men." In these ways, sacred zeal shows itself to be of God and for God.

The Cultivation of Zeal

Christian zeal is not beyond the reach of any saint who sincerely asks it of the Lord and diligently makes use of the means appointed by God for sustaining it. So under God's blessing, what must be done to set our affections ablaze *against* all sinful things and *unto* all holy things? La Belle, drawing from the Puritans, provides five means by which to cultivate such zeal. First, since true zeal is the gift of God, it must be sought by prayer. Ward exhorts, "Pray continually and instantly. The Lord that breathed first your soul into you, will also breathe on your soul." Second, we must attentively and meekly listen to the public preaching of God's Word. Again, Ward says that the fire of zeal must "be preserved fresh by ordinary fuel, especially the priest's lips must keep fire alive. Sermons are bellows ordained for this purpose." Third, we must meditate upon God's glory, our sinfulness, Christ's salvation, and the realities of eternity. Fourth, we must pursue and foster genuine Christian fellowship in the context of the local church. As one Puritan said, "Such as forsake the best fellowship...how can they but take cold? Can one coal alone keep itself glowing?" And fifth, we must be militant and vigilant in our war against indwelling sin. If we would keep a fire in our heart for God, we must take caution not to indulge in any known sin, or neglect any known duty.

Reflect

1. In what ways have you been encouraged and convicted by this lesson? What characteristics of genuine zeal do you see in your own life? Where do you find yourself lacking?

2. Read Psalm 119:136, 139. How does a zealous love for God lead us to react to sin? When was the last time you grieved deeply over your own sin and the sins of those around you?

3. Why does our zeal tend to cool when we do not regularly join the saints in worship? How has God used the public worship of the church to renew your zeal?

Discuss

1. How would you respond to the objection that zealous Christians are too fanatical and intolerant—indeed, too dangerous—and so "moderate Christianity" is better?

2. According to Scripture, there is such a thing as a zeal for God without knowledge (Rom. 10:2). Having seen what genuine, sacred zeal looks like, what are some characteristics of false religious zeal? How can we discern in ourselves whether our zeal is God-honoring or not?

3. La Belle gives reasons why sacred zeal is an absolute necessity for the Christian life. What are the reasons he gives? Can you think of other reasons why such Spirit-wrought passion for God is a nonnegotiable for the Christian?

4. Why would tolerating "small" sins quench your zeal? How should we deal with such violations of God's law in order to fan into flame our love for the righteous God?

Read

Primary Sources

Love, Christopher. *The Zealous Christian: Taking Heaven by Holy Violence in Wrestling and Holding Communion with God in Importunate Prayer.* Morgan, PA: Soli Deo Gloria, 2002.

Owen, John. "Righteous Zeal Encouraged by Divine Protection." In *The Works of John Owen,* 8:133–62. Edinburgh: Banner of Truth Trust, 1991.

Watson, Thomas. *Heaven Taken by Storm: Showing the Holy Violence a Christian Is to Put Forth in the Pursuit after Glory.* Edited by Joel Beeke. Morgan, PA: Soli Deo Gloria, 1992.

Secondary Sources

Beeke, Joel and James La Belle. *Living Zealously.* Grand Rapids: Reformation Heritage Books, 2012.

Murray, Iain H. "The Puritans on Maintaining Spiritual Zeal." In *Adorning the Doctrine,* 72–94. London: Westminster Conference, 1995.

Puritans on Suffering and Providence

Lesson Given by Brian Cosby

Meditate

Question 26 of the Heidelberg Catechism asks, "What believest thou when thou sayest, 'I believe in God the Father, Almighty, Maker of heaven and earth?'" It answers, "That the eternal Father of our Lord Jesus Christ (who of nothing made heaven and earth, with all that is in them; who likewise upholds and governs the same by His eternal counsel and providence) is for the sake of Christ His Son, my God and my Father; on whom I rely so entirely, that I have no doubt but He will provide me with all things necessary for soul and body; and further, that He will make whatever evils He sends upon me, in this valley of tears, turn out to my advantage; for He is able to do it, being Almighty God, and willing, being a faithful Father." Meditate on Psalm 31:19.

Learn

The Puritans embraced the biblical teaching concerning God's exhaustive sovereignty and providential government of all things. Obadiah Sedgwick defined God's providence as "an external action of God whereby He conserves and governs all things wisely, holily, justly, and powerfully, to the admiration of His own glory." He went on to explain that this government "extends to all creatures and the details concerning them."

God's Sovereignty in Suffering

For the Puritans, God's providence encompasses all things, including the suffering of Christians. They believed that all which comes to pass is the working out of God's sovereign will (Eph. 1:11), both the good and the bad. Thomas Brooks, in accord with Psalm 34:19, observed, "God, who is infinite in wisdom and matchless in goodness, hath ordered troubles, yea, many troubles to come trooping in upon us on every side." Christians experience trials and tribulations from the hand of their gracious heavenly Father. Thus, Flavel exhorts us: "In all the sad and afflictive providences that befal you, eye God as the author and orderer of them." The Christian ought to have a God-centered view of suffering, seeing every affliction as from Him, through Him, and unto Him (Rom. 11:36).

God's Purposes in Suffering

But why does God ordain His people to undergo suffering? The Puritans were f ond of referring to suffering as the "school of affliction." God enrolls His children in this school to graciously teach them many lessons. Thomas Boston provides seven potential purposes which the Lord has in painful providences: (1) to prove your spiritual state as a hypocrite or genuine believer; (2) to stir you to obedience, wean you from this world, and set your eyes on heaven; (3) to convict you of sin; (4) to correct or chasten you for sin; (5) to prevent you from committing sin; (6) to reveal latent sin deep within your heart; (7) to awaken you from laziness so that you exercise yourself in grace. In other words, for the Christian, suffering is a "sanctified affliction" which aims at producing holiness (Heb. 12:10). "God's rod," wrote Thomas Watson, "is a pencil to draw Christ's image more lively on us." Because this is so, John Flavel could say, "Let a Christian...be but two or three years without an affliction, and he is almost good for nothing."

Our Response in Suffering

Believing that God's afflictive providences ultimately work out for our good (Rom. 8:28), the Puritans teach us to submit unto God in them. Joseph Caryl put these words into Job's mouth as a model for all believers in affliction (cf. Job 1:20ff.): "Lord, though all this be come upon me, yet I will not depart from thee, or deal falsely in thy covenant. I know thou art still the same Jehovah, true, holy, gracious, faithful, all-sufficient; and therefore behold me prostrate before thee, and resolving still to love thee, still to fear thee, still to trust thee; thou art my God still and my portion forever. Though I had nothing left in the world that I could call mine, yet thou Lord art enough, yet thou alone art all." It is this kind of childlike trust that ought to mark true believers when they walk through the valley of the shadow of death. Such unshaken faith in God is cultivated through the private and public means of grace, especially the Word of God and prayer. "The best posture we can wrestle with afflictions in," said Flavel, "is to engage them upon our knees." Again, he writes that the Bible "must be applied for our comfort in all inward and outward troubles." In this way, we are enabled to endure suffering and to profit optimally from it by God's grace.

Reflect

1. Do you have an aversion to affliction, avoiding it at all costs? How do the Puritans challenge your thinking and disposition toward suffering?

2. Christ, as the Suffering Servant, underwent the most excruciating torment for our sake. How does He teach and enable us to turn outward in service to others in the midst of our suffering? Why are afflictions not an excuse to ignore others and focus solely on ourselves?

3. The Puritans encouraged remembering God's past providences as a means to strengthen faith in the present. How do His past dealings with you give hope for the future and its potential crosses?

Discuss

1. "Godliness cannot secure you from affliction," wrote Flavel, "but it can and will secure you from hell, and sanctify your afflictions to help you to heaven." How would you defend this truth against the errors of health, wealth, and prosperity teaching?

2. How does all suffering, whether undergone by a believer or an unbeliever, lead to the gospel of Jesus Christ? What hope does God provide for sufferers of every kind?

3. What are some examples from biblical and church history of God using immense suffering for immense good in the lives of His people?

4. Expounding Psalm 39:9, Thomas Brooks said, "It is the great duty and concernment of gracious souls to be mute and silent under the greatest afflictions, the saddest providences, and sharpest trials that they meet with in this world." Is it ever proper to vent our questions and struggles to the Lord? How do the Scriptures, especially the Psalms, invite us to honestly pour out our hearts before the Lord without giving way to unsubmissive complaining?

Read

Primary Sources

Flavel, John. *Preparation for Sufferings; Or, The Best Work in the Worst Times. In The Works of John Flavel,* 6:3–83. Edinburgh: Banner of Truth Trust, 1968.

Boston, Thomas. *The Crook in the Lot; Or, The Sovereignty and Wisdom of God in the Afflictions of Men. In The Complete Works of Thomas Boston,* 3:497–590. Stroke-on-Trent: Tentmaker Publications, 2002.

Brooks, Thomas. *The Mute Christian under the Rod.* Grand Rapids: Sovereign Grace, 1971.

Sibbes, Richard. *The Bruised Reed.* Edinburgh: Banner of Truth Trust, 1998.

Secondary Sources

Cosby, Brian. *Suffering & Sovereignty: John Flavel and the Puritans on Afflictive Providence.* Grand Rapids: Reformation Heritage Books, 2012.

Beeke, Joel and Mark Jones. "The Puritans on Providence." In *A Puritan Theology: Doctrine for Life,* 161–77. Grand Rapids: Reformation Heritage Books, 2012.

Puritans on Marriage

Lesson Given by Joel Beeke

Meditate

Henry Smith wrote, "Whereas all other ordinances were appointed of God by the hands of men, or the hands of angels (Acts 12:7; Heb. 2:2), marriage was ordained by God himself [who] cannot err. No man nor angel brought the wife to the husband, but God himself...so marriage hath more honor of God...than all other ordinances of God beside, because He solemnized it Himself." Meditate on Genesis 2:22.

Learn

Unlike the ancient and medieval church, the Puritans possessed a very high view of marriage, rooted in the Scriptures. Thomas Becon defined marriage as a "high, holy and blessed order of life, ordained not of man, but of God, wherein one man and one woman are coupled and knit together in one flesh and body in the fear and love of God, by the free, loving, hearty and good consent of them both, to the intent that they two may dwell together as one flesh and body, of one will and mind, in all honesty, virtue and godliness, and spend their lives in equal partaking of all such things as God shall send them with thanksgiving."

The Purposes of Marriage

The Puritans believed there are three main causes or purposes for which God instituted marriage for His glory.

Companionship

Based upon God's words, "It is not good that the man should be alone" (Gen. 2:18); they argued that marriage was divinely instituted to provide companionship and mutual assistance. Through such companionship, William Perkins said, "the parties married may perform the duties of their callings in a better and more comfortable manner (Prov. 31:11–13)."

Procreation

The Puritans believed that children are a gift of God through which believers are to serve the family, the church, and the state (see Gen. 1:28). William Gouge noted that Christians should have children so "that the world might be increased: and not simply increased, but with a legitimate brood, and distinct families, which are the seminaries of cities and the Commonwealths. Yea also that in the world the Church by an holy seed might be preserved, and propagated (Mal. 2:15)."

Avoidance of Sin

George Swinnock defined marriage as "the lawful conjunction of one man and one woman for the term of their natural lives, for...the avoiding of sin." Marriage is the best and most sanctified solution to the temptation of fornication and adultery.

The Principles of Marriage

According to the Puritans there are two major scriptural principles which are to govern and regulate marriage.

Christ-Church

Ephesians 5:22–33 teaches that the husband is to love his wife as Christ loves the church, and the wife is to show reverence and submission to her husband as the church submits to Christ. The husband is to love his wife absolutely (v. 25), purposefully (v. 26), realistically (v. 27), and sacrificially (vv. 28–29). Such Christlike love, said

Gouge, will serve "as sugar to sweeten the duties of authority which appertain to a husband," and thereby enable his wife to more easily submit to him. Likewise, the wife's submission to her husband parallels the church's submission to Christ. "A wife must submit herself to a husband," Gouge wrote, "because he is her *head*; and she must do it *as unto the Lord*, because her husband is to her, as Christ is to the Church."

Covenant

Marriage is a sacred bond. When a man and a woman exchange the vows of marriage, they are doing more than contracting to share a home and a bank account; they are entering into a covenant with each other with stipulations and responsibilities. Marriage is not only a covenant between husband and wife; it is a *covenant with God* which He witnesses and seals. Henry Scudder therefore advised married couples to "consider what you then did; you then entered into a near covenant with one another, indeed, into a covenant with God to be one another's, and to be faithful to each other.... So that if you break covenant with one another, you break covenant also with your God."

The Practices of Marriage

God, having instituted the marriage bond, has also revealed the duties that are to be carried out within this covenantal union.

Mutual Duties

The ultimate duty to be carried out by both husband and wife is love. "As for love," says William Whately, who wrote two books on marriage, "it is the life, the soul of marriage, without which it is no more itself, than a carcase is a man; yes, it is uncomfortable, miserable, and a living death." Whately describes marital love as "the king of the heart," so that when it prevails, marriage is "a pleasing combination of two persons into one home, one purse, one heart, and one flesh."

Peculiar Duties

Each spouse has unique duties to carry out in the marriage relationship. Matthew Henry summarizes a husband's duties best in saying that the woman is "not made out of his head to rule over him, nor out of his feet to be trampled upon by him, but out of his side to be equal with him, under his arm to be protected, and near his heart to be beloved." Likewise, as a helpmeet for her husband (Gen. 2:18), the wife should assist her husband in a variety of ways, said Smith, helping him "in business, in his labors, in his troubles, in his sickness, like a woman physician."

Reflect

1. The belief that procreation is a chief purpose of marriage runs contrary to the common view of our society that children are an unnecessary inconvenience. Has culture had any effect on the way you view children? If so, in what ways? How do the Scriptures challenge your thinking in this area?

2. Why did the Puritans say that mutual love is the very life of a marriage? Is your life governed by an others-oriented love?

3. How has this lesson challenged your thinking about the institution of marriage? And, whether married or single, how will this change the way you live?

Discuss

1. The Puritans believed that since God instituted marriage, He alone has the right to define it. How does this simple truth deliver us from the man-centered redefining of marriage in our day? Why is it such a serious sin to alter God's definition of holy matrimony?

2. Read Malachi 2:15. What is the Lord seeking through the marriage covenant? What does this reveal about God's purpose for marriage?

3. How have you seen the biblical teachings of headship and submission be distorted? How does the Christ-church principle provide a remedy to such perversions?

4. Why is it important for marriage to be understood as a covenant? What are the implications of the covenantal character of the marriage union?

Read

Primary Sources

Gouge, William. *Building a Godly Home.* Edited by Joel Beeke and Scott Brown. 3 vols. Grand Rapids: Reformation Heritage Books, 2013–2014. (Modernized version of *Domestical Duties*.)

Steele, Richard. "What Are the Duties of Husbands and Wives towards Each Other?" In *Puritan Sermons, 1659–1689,* 2:272–303. Wheaton, IL: Richard Owen Roberts, 1981.

Secker, William. "The Wedding Ring, A Sermon," printed with *The Non-such Professor in His Meridian Spleandour; Or, The Singular Actions of Sanctified Christians,* edited by Matthew Wilks, 245–69. Harrisonburg, VA: Sprinkle, 2009.

Secondary Sources

Bcckc, Joel and James La Belle. *Living in a Godly Marriage.* Grand Rapids: Reformation Heritage Books, 2016.

Ryken, Leland. *Worldly Saints: The Puritans As They Really Were*, 39–54. Grand Rapids: Zondervan, 1986.

Puritans on Family

Lesson Given by Joel Beeke

Meditate

Thomas Cobbett wrote, "The greatest love and faithfulness which parents as cove-nanters can show to God, and to their children, who in and with themselves are joint covenanters with God, is so to educate them, that the conditions of the covenant may be attended by their children, and so the whole covenant fully effected." Meditate on Deuteronomy 6:4–9.

Learn

Joel Beeke states, "Puritan parents were fully engaged with their children throughout their entire growing up, training them, nurturing them, molding them in the fear of God with the realization that on the day of judgment they would have to give an account of their parental stewardship." Below we will look at a few of the covenantal principles that characterized their parenting.

Covenant Sign

With rare exceptions such as John Bunyan, Puritan parenting was rooted in the conviction that children are included in the covenant God makes with believers. This being so, they ought to receive the sign and seal of the covenant. Just as the believing Israelite had to circumcise his son in the old covenant, so, in the new covenant, the Puritans believed that Christians are to baptize children to confirm their inauguration into the covenant of grace. Baxter says that God "ordained baptism to be used as a solemn initiation of all that will come into his church, and enter into the covenant of God." In baptism, Christian parents assume covenant responsibilities on behalf of their children. God therefore claims these children as His own; parents are stewards of their children on God's behalf. But though their children belonged to God, this did not mean their children were viewed as saved from birth. While children of believers are born under the promises of the covenant, they still need to personally appropriate those promises by Spirit-worked faith in Christ alone for salvation.

Covenant Education

The Puritans strove to train their children early in the nurture and admonition of the Lord. They made it a law that parents must teach their children to read so that they could read the Bible and other religious material for their spiritual welfare. Reading opened the world of doctrine to children. Even Puritan reading tools themselves, such as the *New England Primer*, conveyed theology. From this primer, the theological ABCs were taught: from A, "In Adam's Fall, we sinned all," to Z, "Zacchaeus, he did climb the Tree, his Lord to see." The primary goal of the Puritans in the education of their children was not simply a well-stocked head, but a warm appreciation of the truths of God in mind and soul so that the children would lead a holy life. Baxter advises: "Let it be the principle part of your care and labor in all their education to make holiness appear to them the most necessary, honorable, gainful, pleasant, delightful, amiable state of life." The nurturing and training of children was not only to be carried out by teaching, but, more importantly, by example. Richard Greenham writes, "Experience teaches us that children learn more by countenance, gesture, and behavior than by rule, doctrine, precept, or instruction."

Covenant Worship

Family worship was the bedrock of the Puritan family. They would gather to worship the Lord once or twice each day. The Westminster Directory for Family Worship, written by Puritans, states that "family worship, which ought to be performed by every family, ordinarily morning and evening, consists in prayer, reading the Scriptures, and singing praises." First, there was family prayer which was viewed as both a domestic obligation and a privilege. Thomas Brooks said, "A family without prayer is like a house without a roof, open and exposed to all the storms of heaven." Second, there was reading and instruction from the Scripture. William Perkins said that the first component of "household service to God" is "a conference upon the Word of God, for the edification of all the members thereof to eternal life." Fathers should undertake this exercise diligently and with passion. Third, there was the singing of praise to God via the psalms. Such singing promotes devotion as it informs the mind and warms the heart. For the Puritans, daily family worship was a necessity and a privilege. William Whately asserts that a father who does not lead his household in the ways of God through family worship "keeps an household of fiends, a Seminary for the devil, a nursery for hell, and the kingdom of death."

Covenant Discipline

Bringing up children in the fear of the Lord included firm discipline, the Puritans said. "Doctrine and example alone are insufficient," wrote John Norton. "Discipline is an essential part of the nurture of the Lord." Such discipline included both verbal reproof and, when necessary, the rod. On the one hand, the child's naturally evil will must be broken. "Train them up in exact obedience to yourselves, and break them of their own wills," Baxter advised. On the other hand, the Puritans did not want to break a child's spirit in the process of breaking his or her will, and they advocated that discipline be fair, gentle, and geared to the temperament of the child. Parents were to see that their children's stubborn wills and selfishness were restrained and repressed, even as their attractive qualities were commended. Their discipline was pervaded by an optimism that God ordinarily works to save His covenant seed.

Reflect

1. How often do you ponder the significance of your baptism? Do you view your life and family in covenantal terms?

2. If you are a parent, in what ways are you striving by word and example to train your child(ren) in the faith? If you are not a parent, how are you seeking to grow in the graces necessary to be fit for such a task?

3. Were you raised in a home that had daily family worship? From your perspective, what effect did this practice or the lack thereof have on your soul?

_____

_____

_____

_____

_____

_____

_____

_____

_____

_____

_____

Discuss

1. Cotton Mather wrote, "Families are the nurseries for Church and Commonwealth; ruin families and you ruin all." How has this proven true in society today? What is it about the family that makes it so vitally important and foundational?

2. Why did the Puritans baptize their children? Is infant baptism biblical? Why, or why not?

3. What does it mean to catechize? Why is catechesis such an essential part of childrearing? What role, if any, should the catechism play in the life of the church?

4. The word *discipline* has negative connotations in modern culture. How do the Puritans help us to view discipline as a positive ordinance of God? Why is discipline a necessary good for our children?

Read

Primary Sources

Baxter, Richard. *The Godly Home.* Edited by Randall J. Pederson. Wheaton, IL: Crossway, 2010. (Modernized excerpt from *A Christian Directory*.)

Gouge, William. *Building a Godly Home.* Edited by Joel Beeke and Scott Brown. 3 vols. Grand Rapids: Reformation Heritage Books, 2013–2014. (Modernized version of *Domestical Duties*.)

Henry, Matthew. *Family Religion: Principles for Raising a Godly Family.* Fearn, UK: Christian Focus, 2008.

Secondary Sources

Beeke, Joel. *Living for God's Glory: An Introduction to Calvinism*, 333–48. Orlando: Reformation Trust, 2008.

Ryken, Leland. *Worldly Saints: The Puritans as They Really Were*, 39–54. Grand Rapids: Zondervan, 1986.

Puritans on Education

Lesson Given by Leland Ryken

Meditate

Richard Baxter taught that "education is God's ordinary way for the conveyance of his grace, and ought no more to be set in opposition to the Spirit than the preaching of the Word." Mediate on Proverbs 18:15.

Learn

After addressing some common misconceptions, Leland Ryken sets forth the five pillars of Puritan education. Serving as the structure of their promotion of learning, these five pillars provide us with a biblical model for academia today.

The High Value of Education

The Puritans placed a high premium on knowledge and learning, and zealously labored to establish sound schools in their communities. During a Boston synod, John Eliot prayed, "Lord, for schools everywhere among us! Oh, that our schools may flourish! That every member of this assembly may go home and procure a good school to be encouraged in the town where he lives." Such a prayer would sound strange in our churches today, but it was not so in Eliot's day. The Puritans knew how valuable and necessary education was for the good of the church and society. And thus in both England and America, schools multiplied and flourished through their influence. Having established homes, churches, and the civil government, the next thing the newly settled Puritans in America yearned for was "to advance learning and perpetuate it to posterity." They stood strongly against the anti-intellectual tides within the church, expressing the need for a learned ministry, but also the need for a learned laity. Education was for the Puritans not optional but essential.

The Great End of Education

The Puritans understood clearly that the supreme aim of all education is growth in godliness. To know God and to be made like Him is the great end of all of life, and this is no less true with regards to academics. John Milton famously wrote, "The end then of learning is to repair the ruins of our first parents by regaining to know God aright, and out of that knowledge to love him, to imitate him, to be like him." The Puritans stressed that knowledge is an essential and foundational component of true faith and the fruit of faith is a life of obedience to God. Thus, our growth in grace is dependent upon our growth in knowledge. And all of our growth in knowledge ought to find its end in our growth in grace.

The Biblical Foundation of Education

While the Puritans stressed the need for knowledge if one is to have faith, they equally taught that all true knowledge must be founded upon faith. One of the rules of Harvard College in its founding was this: "Let every student be plainly instructed and earnestly pressed to consider well the main end of his life and studies is to know God and Jesus Christ which is eternal life, John 17:3, and therefore to lay Christ in the bottom, as the only foundation of all sound knowledge and learning." Because Christ is the one in whom were hidden all the treasures of wisdom and knowledge (Col. 2:3), the Bible must be central in the world of academia. Cotton Mather asserts that "Scripture is reason in its highest elevation." Every subject of learning was to be subjected to the revelation of God in the Bible. Thomas Hall argued that "we must bring human learning home to divinity to be pruned and pared with spiritual wisdom."

The Classical Content of Education

While the end goal and the foundation of Puritan education was religious in character, its content was the liberal arts. Undergirding their use of a classical curriculum, Ryken claims, was the doctrine of common grace and general revelation. Because God furnishes men, even unbelievers, with gifts of knowledge and morality, Charles Chauncy could write, "Who can deny but that there are found many excellent and divine moral truths in Plato, Aristotle, Plutarch, Seneca, etc.?" And because God reveals Himself in nature, Alexander Richardson wrote, "The world and the creatures therein are like a book wherein God's wisdom is written, and there must we seek it out." This was true of the academic training of ministers of the gospel as well. Richard Bernard asks, "What art or science is there which a divine shall not stand in need of?" He answers that "grammar, rhetoric, logic, physics, mathematics, metaphysics, ethics, politics, economics, history, and military discipline" are all of considerable use to the minister.

The Holistic Purpose of Education

One primary reason the Puritans stressed the liberal arts was because they desired a well-rounded and comprehensive education. Such an education was ideal because it prepared a person for all of life. Robert Cleaver argued that "the more skill and knowledge he hath in the liberal sciences, so much sooner shall he learn his occupation and the more ready shall he be about the same." It not only prepared a person for his or her vocation though, for it also "fits a man," wrote John Milton, "to perform justly, skillfully, and magnanimously, all the offices, both private and public, of peace and war." In other words, such an extensive education equips a person for every sphere of life in society, church, and home.

Reflect

1. Do you value education to the degree that the Puritans did? What in your experience has caused you to have a primarily positive or negative view of academia?

2. John Cotton believed that "knowledge is no knowledge without zeal," however "zeal is but a wild-fire without knowledge." Are you more prone to a zeal without knowledge or a knowledge without zeal? How can both zeal and knowledge be pursued simultaneously and increasingly in your life?

3. The Puritans emphasized the authority of Scripture and Christ in every pursuit of knowledge. Is the Word of God your supreme authority and the foundation of all of your learning? Do you possess a sufficient knowledge of the Bible so as to be able to test all things by it?

Discuss

1. An antinomian minister, in opposition to the Puritans, once said, "I had rather hear such a one that speaks from the mere motion of the spirit, without any study at all, than any of your learned scholars, although he may be fuller of Scripture." Where are similar sentiments being expressed in the church today? How would you respond?

2. Ryken quotes John Preston as saying, "I deny not but a man may have much knowledge and want grace, but on the other side, you cannot have more grace than you have knowledge." Is this an overstatement? Can grace and godliness ever flourish where knowledge is lacking? What is the relationship between knowledge and holiness?

3. The Puritans sought to wed together faith and reason, along with general and special revelation in their understanding of education. How does reason augment faith and faith intensify reason?

4. In what ways do you see the twenty-first-century church implementing these five pillars of Puritan education? Where do you see a present lack and need for growth?

Read

Ryken, Leland. *Worldly Saints: The Puritans as They Really Were*, 157–72. Grand Rapids: Zondervan, 1986.

Miller, Perry. *The New England Mind: The Seventeenth Century.* Cambridge, MA: Belknap Press, 1983.

Cairns, Earle. "The Puritan Philosophy of Education." *Bibliotheca Sacra* 104 (1947): 326–36.

Puritans on Work and Money

Lesson Given by Leland Ryken

Meditate

Cotton Mather wrote, "A Christian should follow his occupation with contentment. It is the singular favor of God unto a man that he can attend his occupation with contentment and satisfaction. Is your business here clogged with any difficulties and inconveniences? Contentment under those difficulties is no little part of your homage to that God who hath placed you where you are." Meditate on Philippians 4:11–13.

Learn

What is the proper place of work and money in the Christian life? The Puritans provide us with a robustly biblical and practical theology of labor and wealth.

The Puritans on Work

Leland Ryken asserts that the Puritan view of work was revolutionary in their day. The stark contrast with medieval Roman Catholicism resulted from the theocentricism (God-centeredness) of the Puritan divines. All legitimate work was ultimately from God, to be carried out by faith in God, to the end of the glory of God.

Work as Vocation

The Puritans believed that each man's work is divinely imposed upon him. Not pastors alone, but every man receives a calling from God, whether a farmer, an architect, or a stay-at-home mother. William Perkins defined vocation as "a certain kind of life, ordained and imposed on man by God, for the common good." He went on to say, "Every person of every degree, state, sex, or condition without exception must have some personal and particular calling to walk in." Because man's work comes from God, it is inherently sacred.

Work as Stewardship

Since God is the one who both calls and equips a person for a particular vocation, each person is responsible before God to carry out his or her work faithfully. Richard Steele exclaimed, "He that hath lent you talents hath also said, 'Occupy till I Come!' How is it that ye stand all day idle? Your trade is your proper province." One's vocation in the world, if it is to be properly stewarded, must be carried out by faith. John Cotton wrote, "A true believing Christian lives in his vocation by his faith. Not only my spiritual life but even my civil life in this world, and all the life I live, is by the faith of the Son of God: He exempts no life from the agency of his faith."

Work as Service

The Puritans viewed work not as an end in itself but as a means to the end of glorifying God. Perkins writes, "The main end of our lives...is to serve God in the serving of men in the works of our callings." It is the glory of God and the good of others that ought to be pursued through our vocations. Thus, all legitimate work ought to be carried out with a humble, servant-hearted disposition toward God and our fellow man.

The Puritans on Money

The Puritans not only had a remarkably different view of work than Roman Catholicism, but also of money. The church of the Middle Ages had enshrined poverty as a virtue. But these English Reformers believed money to be a gift from God that ought to be rightly used for God.

Money as Blessing

Because it is from God, money is inherently good. Baxter wrote, "All love of the creature, the world, or riches is not sin. For the works of God are all good as such." Richard Sibbes agreed that because they are from God, "worldly things are good in themselves and given to sweeten our passage to Heaven."

Money as Dangerous

Though money in itself is a gift from God, the hearts of sinful men quickly turn it into an idol. The Puritans impressed upon their hearers the snare which riches could become unto them. We should pray with Samuel Hieron, "Oh, let not mine eyes be dazzled, nor my heart bewitched with the glory and sweetness of these worldly treasures.... Draw my affection to the love of that durable riches, and to that fruit of heavenly wisdom which is better than gold, and the revenues whereof do surpass the silver, that my chief care may be to have a soul enriched and furnished with Thy grace." These English ministers understood that monetary gain, if it usurped the place of Christ and His spiritual riches in the soul, was lethal.

Money as Stewardship

The key to rightly handling one's riches, according to the Puritans, was to understand the principle of stewardship. Richard Baxter wrote, "As we hold our estates under God, as owner, ruler, and benefactor, so we must devote them to him." God is the ultimate owner of man's wealth and lends it to man as a trust. Money is to be used according to His will and for His glory.

Reflect

1. Seeing that our vocation is from God, we ought to be content in the realm and manner in which God has called us to labor. Are you content in your vocation? Why or why not? How does the God-centeredness of the Puritan view of work help to cultivate contentment?

2. The Puritans saw both work and money as a stewardship from God. Is this your default way of thinking about vocation and finances? Do you see your labor and wealth as lent to you by the Lord as a sacred trust?

3. Ryken says that the Puritans spoke much of the danger of riches, not because money was in itself dangerous but because of sinful man's "excessive devotion to it, false trust in it, and selfish spending of it." Are any of these dispositions toward money present in you? Do you spend as though earthly wealth can satisfy your soul? Do you place your confidence in your bank account?

Discuss

1. Define the Puritan understanding of vocation. What is vocation? And where is such a notion taught in the Scriptures?

2. Ryken says, "Although the Puritans were hard working, they were not workaholics." How did the Puritan view of work deliver them from both under-working (idleness) and over-working (idolatry)?

3. How would you respond to someone who uses James 5:1–5 to argue that money and wealth are inherently evil?

4. In his final sermon, Richard Mather warned, "Experience shows that it is an easy thing in the midst of worldly business to lose the life and power of religion, that nothing thereof should be left but only the external form, as it were the carcass or shell, worldliness having eaten out the kernel, and having consumed the very soul and life of godliness." What is it about worldly wealth and success that so easily ensnare the souls of men?

Read

Primary Sources

Steele, Richard. *The Religious Tradesman*. Hinton, VA: Sprinkle Publications, 1998.

Perkins, William. *A Treatise of the Vocations or Callings of Men.* In *The Work of William Perkins*, ed. Ian Breward, 446–76. Abingdon Berkshire, UK: Sutton Courtenay Press, 1970.

Secondary Sources

Ryken, Leland. *Worldly Saints: The Puritans as They Really Were*, 23–72. Grand Rapids: Zondervan, 1986.

Placher, William. *Callings: Twenty Centuries of Christian Wisdom on Vocation*. Grand Rapids: Eerdmans, 2005.

Helm, Paul. *The Callings: The Gospel in the World*. Edinburgh: Banner of Truth Trust, 1987.

Puritans on Shepherding

Lesson Given by William VanDoodewaard

Meditate

Richard Baxter in his *Reformed Pastor* wrote, "If God would but reform the ministers and set them on their duties zealously and faithfully the people would certainly be reformed. All churches either rise or fall as the ministry doth rise or fall (not in riches and worldly grandeur but) in knowledge, zeal and ability for their work." Meditate on 1 Timothy 4:16.

Learn

According to the Puritans, in the New Testament church, there are three permanent offices: ministers of the Word, elders, and deacons. William Ames wrote that the offices of the church are sufficient to "preserve, propagate and renew the church through regular means" for the glory of God and the Lord Jesus Christ.

The Qualifications of a Shepherd

William Fulke, a contemporary of John Jewel, stated that "England was prevented from experiencing the full fruit of the Reformation because of a preponderance of unlearned and ungodly ministers." The Puritans, perceiving this, sought to examine men by the God-given standard of qualifications set forth in biblical passages such as 1 Timothy 3:1–7 and Titus 1:5–9, requiring aspiring ministers to be both godly and learned.

Godly

For the Puritans, a life of vital godliness was not simply desirous, but absolutely necessary in a pastor. "I confess," wrote Baxter, "that man shall never have my consent to have the charge of other men's souls, and to oversee them in order to their salvation, that takes not heed to himself, but is careless of his own." How could one care for the souls of others who showed no care for his own soul? John Owen said, "If the pastors of [churches]...are not exemplary in gospel obedience and holiness, religion will not be carried on and improved among the people." This godliness was to be evidenced in his marriage, family, and dealings within the broader church and society.

Learned

Not only must the minister be a sanctified man, but he also must be well-educated. Goodwin wrote, "Whereas some men are for preaching only extempore and without study, Paul bids Timothy meditate and study." How can one faithfully teach the flock and rebuke those who contradict the truth (Titus 1:9) if he himself does not possess a deep knowledge of the Scriptures? John Carter, who would later become a Westminster divine, was asked during his ordination exam if he had ever read through the Bible. He replied, "Yes, I have read the Old Testament twice through in the Hebrew, and the New Testament often through in the Greek." Carter was not an anomaly among the Puritans. These men knew their Bibles and strove for a learned ministry.

The Work of a Shepherd

In Bunyan's *The Pilgrim's Progress*, Christian beholds a picture in the Interpreter's House "of a very grave person hang up against the wall, and this was the fashion of it: it had eyes lift up to heaven, the best of books in its hand, the law of truth was written upon its lips, the world was behind its back; it stood as if it pleaded with men, and a crown of gold did hang over its head." Interpreter goes on to explain this to be an image of a faithful gospel minister. The work of such a man, said Baxter, is to employ "a very great care of the Church as a whole and in every part, with great watchfulness and diligence in the use of all those holy actions and ordinances which God hath required us to use for their salvation." As under-shepherds of the Chief Shepherd, ministers share in Christ's prophetic, priestly, and kingly ministry in the church.

Prophet

The shepherd's first task, according to the Puritans, is to feed the sheep with the saving and soul-nourishing Word of God. The primary way this is done is through public preaching, which Richard Bernard defined as "an open unfolding thereof by a public minister to the people's capacity, according to the analogy of faith, with words of exhortation applied to the conscience both to inform and reform, and where they be well, to confirm." But this prophetic ministry is also carried out through evangelism, visitation, and counseling. The pastor is to use every avenue available to him to impress the truths of Scripture upon his people.

Priest

Inseparably connected to the call to feed the flock is the call to intercede on their behalf. The Puritans believed that without prayer, the pastor's preaching, visitation, catechizing, and evangelism would be in vain. Owen wrote, "To preach the word, therefore, and not to follow it with constant and fervent prayer for its success, is to disbelieve its use, neglect its end, and to cast away the seed of the gospel at random." It is also through the priestly work of prayer that the minister's love for his people is fanned into flame.

King

Gospel ministers are called to humbly exercise the kingly authority of Christ in church discipline. The Westminster Confession states that such discipline in necessary "for the reclaiming and gaining of offending brethren, for deterring of others from the like offenses, for purging out of that leaven which might infect the whole lump, for vindicating the honor of Christ, and the holy profession of the gospel, and for preventing the wrath of God, which might justly fall upon the church." Ministers are entrusted with the keys of the kingdom by which they have the authority, under Christ, to grant people entrance into the church and shut people out of the church (Matt. 16:19).

Reflect

1. "All churches either rise or fall," said Baxter, "as the ministry doth rise or fall." If this be the case, how persistently ought you to be in praying for your shepherds? Do you regularly intercede on their behalf?

2. Read Ephesians 4:11–16. Why has God given ministers to His church? What is the relation between ordained gospel ministry and the ministry of every Christian (v. 12)?

3. The Puritans viewed church discipline as a positive ordinance given for the well-being of the church. Do you view church disciple in a primarily positive or negative light? Why is such discipline indispensable for Christ's body?

Discuss

1. Why is a recovery of the biblical qualifications and work of pastors central to the health of the church?

2. How does a church best go about examining a man to see if he has the graces and gifts necessary to be fit for gospel ministry? What practical steps can be taken to guard against ungodly men being ordained to the pastoral office?

3. Why is church membership necessary for the work of shepherding to be carried out?

4. Read Hebrews 13:17. What is entailed in obeying and submitting to elders and ministers? Why is it to the advantage of church members to fulfill this command? According to this passage, how does such submission promote joy among the elders and the members?

Read

Primary Sources

Baxter, Richard. *The Reformed Pastor.* Edinburgh: Banner of Truth Trust, 1974.

Owen, John. "The Ministry the Gift of Christ," "Ministerial Endowments the Work of the Spirit," and "The Duty of a Pastor." In *The Works of John Owen*, 9:431–61. Edinburgh: Banner of Truth Trust, 1965.

Flavel, John. *The Character of a Complete Evangelical Pastor, Drawn by Christ.* In *The Works of John Flavel*, 6:564–85. Edinburgh: Banner of Truth Trust, 1968.

Secondary Sources

Beeke, Joel and Mark Jones. "The Puritans on the Offices of the Church." In *A Puritan Theology: Doctrine for Life*, 641–51. Grand Rapids: Reformation Heritage Books, 2012.

Cook, Paul. "The Life and Work of a Minister According to the Puritans." In *Puritan Papers: Volume One, 1956–1959,* 177–89. Philipsburg, NJ: Presbyterian & Reformed, 2000.

Puritans on Preaching

Lesson Given by Joel Beeke

Meditate

"Preaching," wrote William Ames, "is the ordinance of God, sanctified for the begetting of faith, for the opening of the understanding, for the drawing of the will and affections to Christ." Meditate on Colossians 1:28.

Learn

The era of the Puritan movement has often been called the golden age of preaching. "Preaching, by mouth or by pen," writes John F. N. New, "was life for the Puritan." Through their biblical, doctrinal, experiential, and practical preaching, reformation and revival spread among the people of God.

Primacy of Preaching

The Puritans possessed a very high view of preaching, understanding the authoritative proclamation of the Scriptures to be the primary means God uses to build His church. Thus, according to Robert Traill, preaching is the minister's "principal work" and the hearers' "principal benefit." This necessarily created an ethos where preaching stood at the center of the church's worship and ministry. The Puritans often placed behind their name "Preacher of the Gospel" or "Preacher of the Word," rather than listing their degrees. And the altar, which had for centuries occupied the dominant place in the worship of God's people, was replaced by the pulpit.

Program for Preaching

The Puritans' love for preaching enabled them to focus on establishing an impressive program for comprehensive reform in the church. First, they sought to reform preaching itself to God's revealed will in His Word. Edward Dering said, "The faithful Minister, like unto Christ, [is] one that preacheth nothing but the word of God." Second, they utilized lectureships to advance biblical preaching. Such lecturers had no other ministerial duties, enabling them to devote themselves exclusively to teaching and preaching. Typically, people went to church faithfully to sit through a rather dry morning sermon by a Church of England minister, then went in the afternoon to hear a lecturer powerfully unfold the Scriptures. Third, through prophesyings they cultivated biblical preaching. Such prophesyings were a kind of biblical conference or form of continuing education for ministers. Fourth, they spread biblical preaching far and wide through printed and published sermons. Puritan sermon books were frequently and widely read, and God used them for many conversions and growth in grace of thousands of believers. And fifth, they promoted biblical preaching through ministerial training and education.

Passion for Preaching

The Puritans were passionate about preaching. They loved to preach Christ—biblically, doctrinally, and typologically. "Preaching is the chariot that carries Christ up and down the world," wrote Richard Sibbes. John Flavel said, "The excellency of a sermon lies in the plainest discoveries and liveliest applications of Jesus Christ." They preached the whole Christ to the whole man, offering Him as prophet, priest, and king. But along with their passion for Christ, they also loved the people they preached to and relentlessly sought their conversion and edification. Baxter wrote, "The whole course of our ministry must be carried on in a tender love to our people.... When the people see that you [sincerely] love them, they will hear anything, and bear anything, and follow you the more easily."

Power in Preaching

The preaching of the Puritans powerfully addressed the whole man. First, they addressed the mind with clarity. They believed that our minds must be enlightened by faith and disciplined by the Word, then put to God's service in the world. Second, they confronted the conscience pointedly. As one Puritan wrote, "We must go with the stick of divine truth and beat every bush behind which a sinner hides, until like Adam who hid, he stands before God in his nakedness." They believed such confrontation was necessary because until the sinner gets out from behind that bush, he will never cry to be clothed in the righteousness of Christ. Third, they wooed the heart passionately. Walter Cradock said to his flock, "We are not sent to get galley-slaves to the oars, or a bear to the stake: but He sends us to woo you as spouses, to marry you to Christ."

Plainness in Preaching

The Puritans believed that the best sermons were unadorned, unphilosophical, clear, and pointed. Thomas brooks wrote, "Starched oratory may tickle the brain, but it is plain doctrine that informs the judgment, that convicts the conscience, that bows the will and that wins the heart." The Puritans used the plain style of preaching because they wanted to reach everyone so that all might know the way of salvation. Jonathan Edwards said, "I had rather be fully understood by ten than admired by ten thousand." According to William Perkins, plain preaching generally followed three steps: (1) it gave the meaning of the scriptural passage in its context; (2) it taught a few profitable points of doctrine gathered from the natural sense of the text; and (3) it applied in plain speech the doctrines "rightly collected to the life and manners of men."

Reflect

1. William Ames said, "The receiving of the word consists of two parts: attention of mind and intention of will." Do you often find your mind wandering or your will unmoving under the preaching of God's Word? How could you grow in attentiveness and adherence to the preached Word?

2. An all-consuming love for Christ and His people were the two great passions which undergirded Puritan preaching. How would a growth in such love change how you approached preaching, whether as a minister or as a hearer?

3. The prayerfulness of the Puritans evidenced their utter dependence upon the Spirit of God in preaching. Do you prepare for the Lord's Day with much prayer? Are you conscious of your need of the Spirit while sitting under the preached Word?

Discuss

1. Do you think the Puritans had too high a view of preaching? Does God place the same weight of importance upon preaching in the Scriptures as the Puritans did?

2. The Puritans were discriminatory in their preaching, distinguishing between different types of hearers in their audience and applying the Word accordingly. What are some examples of different classes of hearers in our churches today? Should a preacher try to address every type of hearer in every sermon?

3. "Our people," wrote Jonathan Edwards, "do not so much need to have their heads stored as to have their hearts touched, and they stand in the greatest need of that sort of preaching which has the tendency to do this." How does a preacher reach the hearts of his people? What are some characteristics of the preaching that has most profoundly affected you?

4. The typical Puritan sermon began with an exegetical introduction, looking at the Scripture text in its context for one to three pages, and then launched into a series of doctrines and applications drawn from the text for around ten pages. Is this the best way to preach? How much should the exposition of the text determine and dominate the sermon?

Read

Primary Sources

Perkins, William. *The Art of Prophesying*. Edinburgh: Banner of Truth Trust, 1996.

Edwards, Jonathan. *Altogether Lovely: Jonathan Edwards on the Glory and Excellency of Christ*. Morgan, PA: Soli Deo Gloria, 1997.

Secondary Sources

Beeke, Joel and Mark Jones. *A Puritan Theology: Doctrine for Life*, 681–710. Grand Rapids: Reformation Heritage Books, 2012.

Bridges, Charles. *The Christian Ministry*, 188–343. Edinburgh: Banner of Truth Trust, 1967.

Van Dixhoorn, Chad. *God's Ambassadors: The Westminster Assembly and the Reformation of the English Pulpit, 1643–1653*. Grand Rapids: Reformation Heritage Books, 2017.

Bickel, R. Bruce. *Light and Heat: The Puritan View of the Pulpit*. Morgan, PA: Soli Deo Gloria, 1999.

Puritans on Church and Worship

Lesson Given by Derek Thomas

Meditate

"Worship," wrote Stephen Charnock, "is an act of the understanding, applying itself to the knowledge of the excellency of God, and actual thoughts of his majesty.... It is also an act of the will, whereby the soul adores and reverenceth his majesty, is ravished with his amiableness, embraceth his goodness, enters itself into an intimate communion with this most lovely object, and pitcheth all his affections upon him." Meditate on Psalm 96:1–6.

Learn

According to Derek Thomas, one of the most important legacies of Puritanism was its development of a rigorously biblical theology of public worship. Below we will examine some of the elements of Puritan worship.

Lord's Day Worship

While all of life is to be one of worship to God, the Puritans held that the Lord's Day is especially set apart for the purpose of divine worship. God has given His people one day in seven to devote wholly to His service, in which they not only rest from earthly labors, but gather corporately to render Him the glory due His name. As one Puritan author said, "He that keeps the Sabbath only by resting from his ordinary work, keeps it but as a beast; but rest on this day is so far forbidden as it is an impediment to the outward and inward worship of Almighty God."

Word-Prescribed Worship

The Puritans taught that God has sufficiently revealed His will concerning His worship. Thus, the church ought only to worship God as He has explicitly mandated in His Word. This is often referred to as the regulative principle. The Westminster Confession of Faith states that "the acceptable way of worshiping the true God is instituted by himself, and so limited by his own revealed will, that he may not be worshiped according to the imaginations and devices of men, or the suggestions of Satan, under any visible representation, or any other way not prescribed in the Holy Scripture." The regulative principle, derived from passages such as Deuteronomy 12:32, led to worship that was not only founded upon the Scriptures, but also saturated in the Scriptures.

Simple Worship

The Puritans promoted simplicity in public worship. They sought to do away with the extravagant worship services propounded by Roman Catholics and Anglicans, removing everything that was nonessential. Richard Cox wrote, "I am of the opinion that all things in the church should be pure, simple, and removed as far as possible from the elements and pomps of this world." As they searched the Scriptures they found that the basic elements of corporate worship included reading the Word, praying the Word, singing the Word, preaching the Word, and seeing the Word in the sacraments. John Cotton wrote, "Our principal care and desire is to administer... the ordinances of Christ himself...in their native purity and simplicity, without any dressing or painting of human inventions."

Engaged Worship

Corporate worship was a most serious matter for the Puritans, requiring the active engagement of all of God's people. The Directory for Public Worship exhorts the people "wholly to attend upon it." Regarding the receiving of the preached Word, Richard Baxter instructed, "Make it your work with diligence to apply the word as you are hearing it.... Cast not all upon the minister, as those that will go no further than they are carried as by force.... You have work to do as well as the preaching, and should all the time be as busy as he." But it is not just the preaching of the Scriptures that people ought to be engaged in. As Thomas Adams cautions, "Beloved, mistake not. It is not the only exercise of a Christian to hear a sermon; nor is that Sabbath well spent that dispatcheth no other business for heaven.... God's service is not to be narrowed up in hearing, it hath greater latitude; there must be prayer, praise, adoration." Corporate worship is not a passive matter for God's people, but one which calls forth the whole soul to the rigorous glorification of God.

Spiritual Worship

Such engagement in worship, however, can only be obtained by the blessed influence of the Holy Spirit. True worship is a spiritual exercise wherein our spirits engage with God's Spirit. John Owen explains, "One and the same Spirit discovers the will and worship of God to them all; one and the same Spirit works the same graces for their king in the hearts of them all; one and the same Spirit bestows the gifts that are necessary for the carrying on of gospel worship in the public assemblies." It is by the Spirit that we are carried into communion with all three Persons of the Godhead. Stephen Charnock said, "A spiritual worshipper actually aspires in every duty to know God.... To desire worship as an end, is carnal; to desire it as a means, and act desires in it for communion with God in it, is spiritual, and the fruit of a spiritual life." This belief in the spirituality of worship caused many of the Puritans to reject set liturgies. John Milton strongly asserted that "to imprison and confine by force, into a pinfold of set words, those two most unimprisonable things, our prayers and that Divine Spirit of utterance that moves them, is a tyranny."

Reflect

---

1. Baxter said that the great goals of corporate worship are "the honor of God; the edification of believers; the communicating of spiritual knowledge, holiness, and delight to others; and the increase of God's actual kingdom in the world." Are these the things you pursue when you gather for public worship?

2. Is the simplicity and spiritually of God's worship attractive to you? Are there ways you or your church have succumbed to the seeker-sensitive mentality which seeks to bring elements of the world into worship in order to appeal to unbelievers?

3. Take some time to examine your involvement in corporate worship. Are you fully engaged in glorifying God with His people? Do you receive the Word meekly, pray earnestly, sing joyously, and partake of the sacraments believingly?

Discuss

---

1. What makes worship on the Lord's Day distinct from worship throughout the rest of the week? How does the Lord's Day, as Thomas says, give structure to the Christian life as a whole?

2. Why is the church to only worship God in the ways He has prescribed? What does the regulative principle teach us about the authority of God in His worship?

3. What are some ways simplicity is threatened in the worship of the modern church? Why is such simplicity so difficult to maintain?

4. Is there a place for liturgy in the church's worship? Why, or why not?

Read

Primary Sources

Burroughs, Jeremiah. *Gospel Worship*. Morgan, PA: Soli Deo Gloria, 1990.

Owen, John. "The Nature and Beauty of Gospel Worship." In *The Works of John Owen*, 9:53–84. Edinburgh: Banner of Truth Trust, 1965.

Clarkson, David. "Public Worship to Be Preferred Before Private." In *The Works of David Clarkson*, 3:187–209. Edinburgh: Banner of Truth Trust, 1988.

Secondary Sources

Davies, Horton. *The Worship of the English Puritans*. London: Dacre Press, 1948.

Ryken, Leeland. *Worldly Saints: The Puritans as They Really Were*, 111–34. Grand Rapids: Zondervan, 1986.

Packer, J. I. *A Quest for Godliness: The Puritan Vision of the Christian Life*, 245–57. Wheaton, IL: Crossway, 1990.

Puritans on the Sabbath

Lesson Given by Greg Salazar

Meditate

Thomas Brooks wrote, "There are no Christians in all the world comparable for the power of godliness and heights of grace, holiness, and communion with God, to those who are more strict, serious, studious and conscientious in sanctifying the Lord's Day.... The true reason why the power of godliness is fallen to so low an ebb, both in this and in other countries also, is because the Sabbath is no more strictly and conscientiously observed." Meditate on Isaiah 58:13–14.

Learn

The Puritans' Theology of the Sabbath

"As it is the law of nature, that, in general, a due proportion of time be set apart for the worship of God; so, in his Word, by a positive, moral, and perpetual commandment binding all men in all ages, he hath particularly appointed one day in seven, for a Sabbath, to be kept holy unto him: which, from the beginning of the world to the resurrection of Christ, was the last day of the week; and, from the resurrection of Christ, was changed into the first day of the week, which, in Scripture, is called the Lord's Day, and is to be continued to the end of the world, as the Christian Sabbath" (Westminster Confession 21.7).

Creation

The Puritans held that the Sabbath did not come onto the scene of history with Moses at Mount Sinai, but was a pre-fall creation ordinance given to Adam in the garden

(Gen. 2:1–2). In the fourth commandment, God calls His people to pattern their lives around His manner of working and resting in creation (Ex. 20:8–11). Speaking of this, Jonathan Edwards argued that "mankind should, after [God's] example, work six days, and then rest, and hallow or sanctify the next following; and that they should sanctify every seventh day, or that the space between rest and rest, one hallowed time and another, among his creatures here upon earth, should be six days."

Law

Since the Sabbath is rooted in creation, it is a universal moral standard which stretches from the beginning to the end of history. As Nicholas Bownd reasons, "For so soon as the day was, so soon was it sanctified; that we might know that, as it came in with the first man, so it must not go out but with the last man." Being a part of the law of creation, it was later published at Mount Sinai in the Ten Commandments. This further evidences its abiding validity, argued the Puritans, since the tablets of stone were the inscription of God's moral will for His creatures throughout all time.

Gospel

While the principle of six days of work and one day of rest remains under the gospel, the day itself has changed due to the earth-shattering significance of Christ's resurrection. Bownd writes, "So then they sanctified the last day of the week, because on it God rested from the work of creation; we keep [the first] day, because on it Christ rising from death rested from the work of our redemption; which work of the redemption being a greater work than that of the creation, not only caused a change of the day, but a necessary change of it into this day that we now keep, never to be changed again." This is confirmed by passages such as 1 Corinthians 16:2, Acts 20:7, and Revelation 1:10.

The Puritans' Practice of the Sabbath

"This Sabbath is then kept holy unto the Lord, when men, after a due preparing of their hearts, and ordering of their common affairs beforehand, do not only observe an holy rest, all the day, from their own works, words, and thoughts about their worldly employments and recreations, but also are taken up, the whole time, in the public and private exercises of his worship, and in the duties of necessity and mercy" (Westminster Confession 21.8).

Rest

As God rested from His creative labors on the seventh day and Christ rested from His redemptive labors on the first day, so too the Lord's Day is to be a day devoted to rest from our ordinary labors. Such rest does not denote laziness, for as John Owen said, "Idleness is a sin every day: but much more on the Lord's Day." Rather God calls us to rest, writes Bownd, because "we cannot attend God's business if we are encumbered with worldly business."

Worship

"The Sabbath," wrote Matthew Henry, "was made a day of rest, only in order to its being a day of holy work, a day of communion with God, a day of praise and thanksgiving; and the rest from worldly business is therefore necessary, that we may closely apply ourselves to this work, and spend the whole time in it, in public and private." For the Puritans, this was the grand purpose of the Sabbath—public, family, and private worship.

Delight

A day devoted to the worship of God was to the Puritans a taste of heaven on earth. As George Swinnock said, "Joy suits no person so much as a saint, and it become no season as well as a Sabbath." He later praised the Lord's Day, writing, "Hail thou that art highly favored of God, thou golden spot of the week, thou market-day of souls, thou daybreak of eternal brightness, thou queen of days, the Lord is with thee, blessed art thou among days.... Oh the mountings of mind, the ravishing happiness of heart, the solace of soul, which on thee [God's people] enjoy in the blessed Saviour!"

Reflect

1. John Owen warned of the errors of legalism and antinomianism when approaching the Sabbath. Do you find yourself more prone to construct manmade rules (legalism) or to reject God-given principles (antinomianism) for the Sabbath? How does the gospel deliver from both of these errors?

2. The Puritans took delight in the Sabbath as their God-given duty. What is the relationship between God's law and your joy? Do you delight in the Lord's Day?

3. John Dod wrote, "If ever we will make good markets for our souls, we must be preparing our hearts...that we may then be burdened with no sin nor worldly care." Do you take time to prepare your heart for the Lord's Day? What practical steps could you take to better ready yourself in body and soul for this Day of days?

Discuss

---

1. Why is the right keeping of the Lord's Day so integral to a life of godliness? Did the Puritans overstate their case when they argued that a Christian's usefulness is in a large measure determined by his adherence to the fourth commandment?

2. What did the Puritans mean when they spoke of the Sabbath as "the market day of the soul"?

3. How does one understand passages such as Romans 14:5 and Colossians 2:16–17 in light of the abiding validity of the Sabbath?

4. The Westminster Confession, teaching that the Lord's Day is to be devoted to God's worship, does make room for "duties of necessity and mercy." What is to be included under this category?

Read

Primary Sources

Bownd, Nicholas. *The True Doctrine of the Sabbath*. Grand Rapids: Reformation Heritage Books, 2015.

Owen, John. *A Day of Sacred Rest*. In *The Works of John Owen*, 18:265–546. Edinburgh: Banner of Truth Trust, 1968.

Ames, William. *The Marrow of Theology*, 287–300. Grand Rapids: Baker, 1997.

Secondary Sources

Dennison, James T. *The Market Day of the Soul: The Puritan Doctrine of the Sabbath in England, 1532–1700*. Lanham, MD: University Press of American, 1983.

Beeke, Joel and Mark Jones. "John Owen on the Christian Sabbath and Worship." In *A Puritan Theology: Doctrine for Life*, 653–79. Grand Rapids: Reformation Heritage Books, 2012.

Kenneth L. Parker, *The English Sabbath: A Study of Doctrine and Discipline from the Reformation to the Civil War*. Cambridge: Cambridge University Press, 1988.

Puritans on Evangelism and Missions

Lesson Given by Joel Beeke

Meditate

Joseph Alleine wrote in his classic *An Alarm to the Unconverted*, "All of Christ is accepted by the sincere convert. He loves not only the wages but the work of Christ, not only the benefits but the burden of Christ.... He takes up the commands of Christ, yea, the cross of Christ. The unsound convert takes Christ by halves. He is all for the salvation of Christ, but he is not for sanctification. He is for the privileges, but does not appropriate the person of Christ. He divides the offices and benefits of Christ. This is an error in the foundation. Whoever loves life, let him beware here. It is an undoing mistake, of which you have often been warned, and yet none is more common." Meditate on Matthew 7:21–23.

Learn

Although the word *evangelism* is scarcely found in their writings, the Puritans were a profoundly evangelistic people. When we speak of "Puritan evangelism," we mean the Puritans' proclamation of the truth of God's Word regarding the salvation of lost men from sin and its consequences in Christ.

Their Message in Evangelism

The evangelistic message of the Puritans consisted of the weighty truths of God revealed in the Scriptures.

God

They proclaimed God's majestic being, His trinitarian personality, and His glorious attributes. All of their evangelism was rooted in a robust biblical theism, unlike modern evangelism which too often approaches God as if He were a next-door neighbor who can adjust His attributes to our needs and desires. The Puritans understood that the doctrines of atonement, justification, and reconciliation are meaningless apart from a true understanding of the God who condemns sin, atones for sinners, justifies them, and reconciles them to Himself.

Sin

The Puritans were not afraid to call sin *sin*, declaring it to be moral rebellion against God which reaps eternal guilt. They preached about sins of commission and sins of omission in thought, word, and deed. They stressed that the problem of sinners was twofold: a bad record, which is a legal problem; and a bad heart, which is a moral problem. Both make us unfit for communion with God. More than an outward reformation of life is needed to meet the demands of God; inward regeneration of heart through the triune God is essential for salvation (John 3:3–7).

Christ

Preaching Christ with winsomeness and grace was the greatest burden and most essential task of the Puritan evangelist. Robert Traill said, "Christ crucified" must be "the subject matter of gospel-preaching." Robert Bolton agreed, "Jesus Christ is offered most freely, and without exception of any person, every Sabbath, every Sermon." They consistently presented Christ in His ability, willingness, and preciousness as the only Redeemer of lost sinners.

Their Methods for Evangelism

The primary methods of Puritan evangelism were plain preaching and catechetical teaching. Through these vehicles they brought the Word of Christ to bear upon hell-worthy sinners.

Preaching

The Puritans believed evangelism was to be foremost carried out through the pulpit. In their sermons, they sought to address the whole soul of the unbeliever with the whole Word in order that they might flee to Christ for refuge. William Ames wrote, "Preaching, therefore, ought not to be dead, but alive and effective so that an unbeliever coming into the congregation of believers should be affected and, as it were, transfixed by the very hearing of the word so that he might give glory to God."

Catechizing

The Puritans believed that pulpit messages should be reinforced by personalized ministry through catechesis—the instruction in fundamental Christian doctrines via questions and answers supported by Scripture. Matthew Henry said of the Westminster Shorter Catechism, "By these forms of sound words the main principles of Christianity, which lie scattered in Scripture, are collected and brought together." Through the personal one-on-one work of catechizing, they impressed the Word of God upon the consciences and hearts of their people to the end that they might come to Christ and grow in grace.

Their Disposition in Evangelism

The Puritan evangelist possessed a sense of dependency on the Holy Spirit coupled with a life of prayerfulness.

Dependence

They felt keenly their inability to bring anyone to Christ, as well as the magnitude of conversion. William Gurnall said to ministers, "God never laid it upon thee to convert those he sends thee to. No; to publish the gospel is thy duty." The Puritans were convinced that both preacher and listener are totally reliant on the work of the Spirit to effect regeneration and conversion when, how, and in whom He will. John Owen said that the Spirit's regenerating action is "infallible, victorious, irresistible, and always efficacious"; it "removeth all obstacles, overcomes all oppositions, and infallibly produces the effect intended."

Prayer

The Puritans saturated all their evangelistic efforts in prayer. They were effective evangelists only because they were also great petitioners who wrestled with God for divine blessing upon their preaching. Richard Baxter said, "Prayer must carry on our work as well as preaching; he preacheth not heartily to his people, that prayeth not earnestly for them. If we prevail not with God to give them faith and repentance, we shall never prevail with them to believe and repent."

Reflect

1. The Puritans boldly told men of their native depravity and of God's unspotted holiness. In your evangelism do you tend to blunt the sharp edges of these biblical truths? To what extent is your speech to the unconverted pervaded with Scripture?

2. The true convert, said Alleine, "is willing to have Christ upon any terms; he is willing to have the dominion of Christ as well as deliverance by Christ." Have you bowed the knee to Christ as your sovereign King? Why is it that Christ cannot be your Savior without also being your Lord?

3. Do you ever find yourself fearful to share the gospel with the unconverted? What does this reveal about your dependence upon God and confidence in His power?

Discuss

1. What differences do you see between Puritan evangelism and modern-day evangelism? In what ways does the twenty-first-century church need reform in this area?

2. Is there ever a danger of focusing too much on sin in evangelism? How much conviction does one have to evidence before we call him or her to Christ?

3. Puritan evangelism was discriminatory, applying Scripture to the souls of men to help them see whether they were in Christ or in Adam. How could the beatitudes in Matthew 5:3–12 be used in this way? What other portions of Scripture would be useful in helping someone discern their spiritual condition before God?

4. Why does the doctrine of God's sovereignty in salvation (i.e., Calvinism) produce a profound God-centeredness and God-dependence in evangelism? How do the doctrines of grace drive us to pray for the advancement of Christ's kingdom?

Read

Primary Sources

Baxter, Richard. *The Reformed Pastor*. Edinburgh: Banner of Truth Trust, 1974.

Alleine, Joseph. *An Alarm to the Unconverted*. Evansville, IN: Sovereign Grace, 1959.

Baxter, Richard. *A Call to the Unconverted*. Wilmington, DE: Sovereign Grace, 1972.

Secondary Sources

Beeke, Joel. *Puritan Evangelism: A Biblical Approach*. Grand Rapids: Reformation Heritage Books, 2012.

Packer, J. I. "The Puritan View of Preaching the Gospel." In *Puritan Papers*, *Vol. 1, 1956–1959*. Phillipsburg, NJ: P&R, 2000.

Rooy, Sidney. *The Theology of Missions in the Puritan Tradition*. Grand Rapids: Eerdmans, 1965.

Puritans on Awakening and Revival

Lesson Given by John Snyder

Meditate

Jonathan Edwards, referring to the New England revival, wrote, "When God manifests himself with such glorious power, in a work of this nature, he appears especially determined to put honor upon his Son, and to fulfil his oath that he has sworn to him, that he would make every knee to bow...to him. God hath had it much on his heart, from all eternity, to glorify his dear and only-begotten son; and there are some special seasons that he appoints to that end, wherein he comes forth with omnipotent power to fulfil his promise...to him." Meditate on Psalm 85:6.

Learn

The Puritans are not typically thought of as preachers of revival. The term is scarcely found in their writings, save those of Jonathan Edwards. But while not writing extensively on the theme, the Puritans were men in pursuit of revival and men who experienced it. J. I. Packer goes so far as to say, "For a truly adequate understanding of Puritanism we must await the day when its history will be told as a revival history.... Puritanism was, at its heart, a movement of spiritual revival." The great aim of these men was to see the church revitalized and enlivened by the Holy Spirit.

Iain Murray perceptively remarks, "In any biblical revival the norm is heightened; it is not suspended while another type of Christianity is introduced." In such times of renewal, God blesses the ordinary means of preaching and prayer in an extraordinary manner. Edwards describes revival as "remarkable effusions at special seasons of mercy" wherein "God appears unusually present." Elsewhere, he explains that

"Though there be a more constant influence of God's Spirit always in some degree attending His ordinances, yet the way in which the greatest things have been done towards carrying on this work always has been by remarkable effusions at special seasons of mercy." God is always present when His people are gathered and His Word is preached, but in these extraordinary times, He comes in a truly remarkable way to bless His people. The result is not a new kind of Christianity but a heightened experience of true Christianity.

The Puritans, though writing little on the subject of revival, knew God's reviving grace in their personal experience and ministries. Their churches knew of these "remarkable effusions" of the Holy Spirit. Below we will examine some of the marks of true, biblical revival as exhibited in the Puritans.

Increased Prayer

Prayer is where revival always begins. Edwards wrote, "So is God's will, through his wonderful grace, that the prayers of his saints should be one great and principal means of carrying on the designs of Christ's kingdom in the world. When God has something very great to accomplish for his church, it is his will that there should precede it the extraordinary prayers of his people.... And it is revealed that, when God is about to accomplish great things for his church, he will begin by remarkably pouring out the spirit of grace and supplication." It is not surprising that many of the men God greatly used during the Puritan era were men of unusual devotion in the secret place.

Increased Hunger

Where God's Spirit is awakening and reviving, there will be an increased desire for and delight in the ordinary means of grace, especially the preaching of the Word. We find in sixteenth- and seventeenth-century England an insatiable hunger for preaching. Laurence Chaderton, having preached for two hours straight, said to his congregation, "I will no longer trespass upon your patience." To which the congregation exclaimed, "For God's sake, go on, go on." Henry Smith's church was often so crowded on the

Lord's Day that "persons of quality, as well as others, were frequently obliged to stand in the aisles." It is recorded of John Bunyan that "about twelve hundred come to hear him preach at a morning lecture at seven o'clock, on a working day, in the dark winter-time." During seasons of revival, God's Spirit draws His people to the ordinary means with an unremittent, unquenchable hunger.

Increased Conversions

When God visits His church with revival, the inevitable result is always an increased number of people being converted to Christ. One historian writes of John Stock that "great numbers were converted, comforted, and established under his ministry." Similarly, it was said of the ministry of William Gouge that "thousands were converted and built up under his ministry." The seventeenth-century Scottish preacher John Livingstone recorded the divine blessing in his own day: "Through the whole land, excepting the professed Papists, and some few who adhered to the prelates, people universally entered into the covenant of God." Read the lives of the Puritans and you will find men whose preaching was extraordinarily blessed by God's Spirit unto the salvation of many souls.

Increased Assurance

Revival, however, did not simply mean an increase in conversions, but also an increase of assurance for those already in Christ. In such times, when the Spirit is mightily poured out, the faith of believers is strengthened and their experience of God's love deepened. William Guthrie described the witness of the Spirit as "a glorious divine manifestation of God unto the soul, shedding abroad God's love in the heart. It is a thing better felt than spoke of.... O how glorious is this manifestation of the Spirit! Faith here riseth to so full an assurance that it resolveth wholly into the sensible presence of God." Richard Sibbes wrote, "This witness of the Spirit is known from the strong conviction it bringeth with it, which weigheth and overpowers the soul to give credit unto it." In revival, God comes in His powerful grace and makes His people to know that they are His. And such assurance leads necessarily to holiness of life.

Reflect

1. How would you define revival? Can you give examples from biblical history of such awakening among God's people?

2. Have you grown complacent and content with infrequent conversions, little hunger for God's ordinances, or weak assurance of salvation in the church?

3. What conditions in your own soul and church evidence the necessity of revival? Does your prayer life show that you have been gripped by this sense of need?

Discuss

1. Martyn Lloyd-Jones said, "You cannot stop a revival any more than you can start it. It is altogether in the hands of God." How does this differ from the prevailing understanding of revival today? Why can't we manufacture revival and put it on our calendars?

2. If revival is fully a work of divine grace, why are we so prone to exalt the men God uses in it? How ought revival to produce humility in God's people?

3. What role do corporate prayer meetings play in revival? Ought the church to place more emphasis on the importance of gathering together to seek God's face?

4. John Snyder referred to "the unfulfilled promises of Scripture" which Christians ought to plead when praying for revival. What are some examples of such promises? What encouragements do the Scriptures give us to pray for awakening?

Read

Edwards, Jonathan. *A Treatise Concerning Religious Affections. In The Works of J onathan Edwards*, 1:234–343. Edinburgh: Banner of Truth Trust, 1974.

Edwards, Jonathan. *Thoughts on the Revival of Religion in New England. In The Works of Jonathan Edwards*, 1:365–430. Edinburgh: Banner of Truth Trust, 1974.

Kang, Mun Jin. "Puritanism and Revival." ThM thesis, University of Glamorgan, 2000.

Packer, J. I. *A Quest for Godliness: The Puritan Vision of the Christian Life*, 309–27. Wheaton, IL: Crossway, 1990.

Lloyd-Jones, D. Martyn. *The Puritans: Their Origins and Successors*, 1–23. Edinburgh: Banner of Truth Trust, 1987.

Puritans on Politics and Culture

Lesson Given by Greg Salazar

Meditate

In his famous work entitled *The Character of an Old English Puritan*, John Geree writes, "He accounted subjection to the higher powers to be part of pure religion... yet did he distinguish between authority and lusts of magistrates, to that he submitted, but in these he durst not be a servant of men, being bought with a price. Just laws and commands he willingly obeyed not only for fear but for conscience also; but such as were unjust he refused to observe, choosing rather to obey God than man; yet his refusal was modest and with submission to penalties, unless he could procure indulgence from authority." Meditate on Acts 5:29.

Learn

Reforming by the Word of God

The Puritans were desirous of bringing all of life under the lordship of Christ. They, thus, sought reform, not only within the church, but in the wider cultural and political scene. This pursuit was rooted in their belief that God rules over the kingdoms of this world and that His Word is authoritative in all spheres of life. They believed, said Geree, that Christianity ought to produce the "best husbands, best wives, best parents, best children, best masters, best servants, best magistrates, best subjects, that the doctrine of God might be adorned, not blasphemed." All men in all spheres of service are to regulate all their affairs by the Word of God, including monarchs and members of parliament. They longed to see a culture in England that honored God and was regulated by His law.

Reforming by Political Means

The Puritans were not afraid to pursue reformation in the church by means of the English government. In their time, the King or Queen was viewed as the supreme head of the church. Though they denied that Christ's church was ultimately subject to an earthly monarch, the Puritans winsomely sought to advance the reformation cause by persuading political authorities to carry it out.

One classic example of this is *The Admonition to Parliament*, in which the Puritans expressed their concern over many of the unbiblical practices of the church of England, calling upon Parliament to implement reform. Near the conclusion of this work, these ministers wrote, "If it might please her Majesty, by the advice of your Right Honorable, in this High Court of Parliament, to hear us by writing or otherwise to defend ourselves, then, such is the equity of our cause that we would trust to find favor in her Majesty's sight." But while the Puritans sought the favor of the political authorities in their reforming work, they were not willing to compromise in order to get it. They continued, "If this cannot be obtained, we will, by God's grace, address ourselves to defend his truth by suffering and willingly lay our heads to the block, and this shall be our peace, to have quiet consciences with our God, whom we will abide for with all patience until he work our full deliverance." These men were willing to seek reform by means of political favor, but they had no desire for political favor at the expense of reformation.

Reforming by Diplomatic Means

Many Puritans remained in the Church of England despite their concerns over certain institutions imposed by the Book of Common Prayer. They believed that, unlike the Roman Catholic Church, the Church of England was a true church. And they resolved to continue ministering in her so long as they had the freedom to preach the Word. To remain in the Church of England, however, required great tact and wisdom (what Greg Salazar calls "diplomatic sensibilities"). It would entail a certain degree of conformity in things like wearing the required vestments, accepting an episcopal form of church government, and not publically denouncing the errors of the English Church.

Those who remained in the Church of England did so with a clean conscience. Though they disapproved of the robes worn by English clergy, they were willing to wear the clerical vestments if it meant they could preach the Word of God to the people of God. Though they were by-and-large Presbyterian in their form of church government, they were willing to remain within an episcopal hierarchy. Though they had serious disagreements with the church, they were willing not to publish them, or in some cases to publish them anonymously. For them, if this measure of conformity was required to pursue reform in the Church of England, then they would gladly undergo it for the sake of Christ's cause.

They, however, were not willing to violate their conscience. The Puritan conscience was bound by the Word of God. Sir Robert Harley described a Puritan as "one that dares do nothing in the worship of God or course of his life but what God's word warrants him, and dares not leave undone anything that the word commands him." They were not willing to compromise the preaching of God's Word and the worship on God's day for the sake of remaining within the Church of England. For example, when Charles I required *The Book of Sports*, a work that denigrated a biblical view of the Sabbath, to be read from the pulpits of all English churches, many Puritans suffered suspension for their refusal to read it. At the end of the day, the Puritans were bound to the Word of God and were not willing to subject God's Word to the will of men.

Reflect

1. The Puritans possessed a vision for reform that encompassed all things. Do you have such a passion to see all of life brought into submission to God? How can you seek to advance Christ's cause in the various spheres which He has called you to serve (e.g., family, church, work, community, etc.)?

2. Read Romans 13:1. Do you show respect and submission toward the governing authorities, even when you disagree with their actions or beliefs?

3. For the sake of truth, the Puritans said they would "willingly lay [their] heads to the block." Are you willing to die for God's truth? How is such a bravery and willingness cultivated?

_____

_____

_____

_____

_____

_____

_____

_____

Discuss

1. Why does God's Word have authority, not only in the church, but in the world? What does a culture shaped by God's Word look like?

2. Is it possible for one to conform to something he disagrees with without violating his conscience? How did the Puritans exemplify this to the glory of God?

3. Are there ways that the political sphere can be used today to advance reformation?

4. In what areas is the church pressured to compromise God's truth by the current political and cultural scene? How does the Word of God speak to these issues?

Read

Capp, Bernard. *England's Culture Wars: Puritan Reformation and Its Enemies in the Interregnum, 1649–1660*. Oxford: Oxford University Press, 2012.

Durston, Christopher and Jacqueline Eales, eds. *The Culture of English Puritanism, 1560–1700*. London: Macmillan Press, 1996.

Packer, J. I. *A Quest for Godliness: The Puritan Vision of the Christian Life*, Wheaton, IL: Crossway, 1990.

Puritans on Paedobaptist Covenant Theology

Lesson Given by Mark Jones

Meditate

Francis Roberts refers to the promise of Genesis 3:15 as "the first and most ancient gospel recorded in the Bible." Meditate on this promise and its unfolding in redemptive history.

Learn

"The English Puritans," notes Mark Jones, "by and large believed that all true theology was based on some form of a divine covenant." But what exactly did they understand a covenant to entail? John Owen defines a covenant as "a convention, compact, and agreement for some certain ends and purposes between the holy Creator and his poor creatures." The Puritans spoke with one accord of covenant as a mutual agreement between two unequal parties. Below we will look at what the Westminster Confession teaches concerning the major covenants set forth in Scripture.

The Covenant of Works

"The first covenant made with man was a covenant of works, wherein life was promised to Adam; and in him to his posterity, upon condition of perfect and personal obedience" (Westminster Confession 7.2).

Reward

The divines begin by emphasizing the gracious promise of God to Adam. But where do we read of a promised reward in the Garden of Eden? The Puritans saw it implicitly revealed in the divine threat "you shall surely die" (Gen. 2:17). If the promised curse for disobedience was death, then the promised blessing for obedience was life.

Headship

This promise of life was given, not only to Adam, but "to his posterity." Drawing from texts like Romans 5:12–21, the Puritans believed Adam to be the covenant head of humanity. Thus, Edmund Calamy wrote that Adam receives a "Covenant both for himself and all his posterity.... He breaking that Covenant brought not only guilt upon himself but upon all his posterity with him."

Condition

The covenantal promise made to Adam and his seed was conditioned upon his "perfect and personal obedience" to God. Having the law written upon his heart in creation and having received the positive command not to eat of the tree of knowledge of good and evil (Gen. 2:16–17), Adam's blessed estate was dependent upon his obedience.

The Covenant of Redemption

"It pleased God, in his eternal purpose, to choose and ordain the Lord Jesus, his only-begotten Son, to be the Mediator between God and men...unto whom he did, from all eternity, give a people to be his seed, and to be by him in time redeemed, called, justified, sanctified, and glorified" (Westminster Confession 8.1).

Appointment

The Puritans stressed that the Father appointed the Son to the office of Mediator in the eternal "Counsel of peace" (Zech. 6:13; or covenant of redemption) established between them. And this appointment Christ voluntarily took up. Texts such as John 6:27, 1 Peter 1:20, and Isaiah 42:6, said Patrick Gillespie, make plain that Christ "was by an eternal act of God's will called to this work, and that long before he came into the world."

Seed

In this covenant arrangement, Christ was given a particular people for whom He would function as Mediator. Christ undertook the office of Redeemer, not for all, but for His chosen ones (John 17:3, 6, 9, 11).

Fulfilment

That which is purposed in eternity between the Father and the Son comes to fruition in time. For, as Samuel Rutherford said, "The Son is decreed...to be in time clothed with our nature, and to put on the state and legal condition of a Covenant-Obeyer of God to the death." Christ, in His incarnation, subjected Himself to the law and perfectly fulfilled it in His life and death as the covenant head of His people.

The Covenant of Grace

"Man by his fall having made himself incapable of life by that covenant, the Lord was pleased to make a second, commonly called the Covenant of Grace; whereby he freely offereth unto sinners life and salvation by Jesus Christ, requiring of them faith in him, that they may be saved.... This covenant was differently administered in the time of the law, and in the time of the gospel" (Westminster Confession 7.3,5).

One Savior

The Puritans taught that subsequent to the fall, all men were saved only through Spirit-worked faith in the Mediator Jesus Christ. Old Testament saints like Adam, Abraham, and David were redeemed from their sin in the same manner as New Testament saints, namely by faith in the gospel, apart from works of the law. Christ is central in the salvation of His people throughout all time.

One People

Believers under the old economy partook of the same covenant of grace as those under the new, and thus formed a singular people of God. Through faith, Jews and Gentiles comprise one family of sinners united to the same Savior.

Progressive Revelation

God first set forth the covenant of grace in Genesis 3:15, and with each subsequent covenant He further revealed His plan of salvation to His people. What was foretold by prophecy and signified by types under the law is fulfilled by Christ and His redemptive work under the gospel. John Owen writes, "That covenant which had invisibly, in the way of a promise, put forth its efficacy under types and shadows, was now solemnly sealed, ratified, and confirmed, in the death and resurrection of Christ." In short, the covenant of grace worked out in time is of one essence with the covenant of redemption established from eternity. That's why some Puritans viewed these covenants as one: the covenant of grace from eternity and the covenant of grace in time.

Reflect

1. Read Ephesians 1:4. Do you tend to think of election as an impersonal matter? How does the covenant of redemption make Christ central in election?

2. The concept of federal headship emerges in both the covenant of works and the covenant of grace. What are the implications of being in Adam or in Christ? Do you consider these categories to be fundamental to your identity? Which person are you in?

3. How does understanding the progressive unfolding of the covenant of grace inform your reading of the Bible? How is biblical revelation marked by both unity and diversity? Explain the difference between promise and fulfillment, as well as shadow and reality.

Discuss

1. Why do you think the Puritans stressed the idea of "mutual agreement" in their definition of covenant? Were they correct in understanding divine covenants in this way?

2. All mankind fell in Adam, as he is the covenant representative of humanity. Thus, we are all born guilty under a broken covenant of works. How would you respond to objections that this is unfair?

3. The covenant of redemption, writes Herman Witsius, "is the foundation of the whole of our salvation." How is this so? And how does this magnify the triune God in our salvation?

4. Mark Jones explains how the Puritans took great care in speaking of the covenant of grace as *conditional*. Why is it important to be balanced when referring to covenant conditions? How can imbalance here lead to antinomianism, legalism, or Arminianism?

Read

Primary Sources

Boston, Thomas. *The Covenant of Works* (vol. 11) and *The Covenant of Grace* (vol. 8). In *The Complete Works of Thomas Bosto*n. 12 vols. Stoke-on-Trent, England: Tentmaker Publications, 2002.

Henry, Matthew. *The Covenant of Grace*. Fearn, UK: Christian Focus, 2002.

Witsius, Herman. *The Economy of the Covenants between God and Man*. 2 volumes. Grand Rapids: Reformation Heritage Books, 2010.

Secondary Sources

Beeke, Joel and Mark Jones. *A Puritan Theology: Doctrine for Life*, 217–78. Grand Rapids: Reformation Heritage Books, 2012.

Woolsey, Andrew. *Unity and Continuity in Covenantal Thought*. Grand Rapids: Reformation Heritage Books, 2012.

Seventeenth-Century Baptist Covenant Theology

Lesson Given by Jeremy Walker

Meditate

Charles Spurgeon, ministering more than two centuries after many of the Puritans, wrote, "The doctrine of the covenant lies at the root of all true theology. It has been said that he who well understands the distinction between the covenant of works and the covenant of grace, is a master of divinity. I am persuaded that most of the mistakes which men make concerning the doctrines of Scripture are based upon fundamental errors with regard to the covenants of law and grace." Meditate on Romans 5:17.

Learn

Though a minority in number, some Puritan ministers and theologians eventually rejected their previous practice of baptizing the infants of believing parents. They believed that the covenant theology undergirding paedobaptism (infant baptism), while possessing much truth, was not fully consistent with the Word of God. Their covenant theology, in which they believed that those inconsistencies were resolved, resulted in the belief that only professing believers should receive the sacrament of baptism.

Agreement Affirmed

While possessing important differences, the covenant theology of Puritan Baptists was in fundamental agreement with much of that of their paedobaptist brothers.

Covenant of Redemption

The Second London Baptist Confession 7.3 states that the covenant of grace "is founded in that eternal covenant transaction that was between the Father and the Son about the redemption of the elect." Using identical language to that found in the Westminster Standards, the following chapter affirms, "It pleased God, in his eternal purpose, to choose and ordain the Lord Jesus, his only begotten Son, according to the covenant made between them both, to be the mediator between God and man."

Covenant of Works

Puritan Baptists also agreed with fellow paedobaptist ministers in their understanding of the covenant of works. Nehemiah Coxe wrote, "As to the terms and condition of this covenant that God made with Adam and all mankind in him, it was a covenant of works.... Therefore the corruption of fallen Adam and the guilt of his fall were derived from him to all his offspring because they were in him as a public person and federal root when he fell."

Covenant of Grace

The Baptists who rose out of Puritanism hold to a distinct understanding of how the covenant of grace related to the covenants God made with Israel. They still stressed the unity of this covenant and the fact that there was only one way of salvation throughout redemptive history. The seventeenth-century Particular Baptist John Spilsbury affirmed, "The Church of God under the old Testament, and that now under the new, for nature are one, in reference to the Elect of God, called to the faith, and by the Spirit of grace united to Christ, as the branches to their vine."

Disagreement Asserted

While there was significant agreement among Puritan-minded Baptists and paedobaptists, there were serious points of disagreement which had important implications for whether children of believers were included in the covenant community and received the sign of the covenant (baptism). The two main areas where Baptists departed from paedobaptist covenant theology were in their understanding of the Abrahamic and new covenants.

Abrahamic Covenant

Though most Puritan-minded Baptists denied that the covenant made with Abraham was itself the covenant of grace, they connected it closely to the covenant of grace. Coxe wrote, "Despite the relationship this covenant has to the covenant of grace, it yet remains distinct from it." While the covenant of grace was promised in the Abrahamic covenant, that covenant also entailed physical and temporal promises pertaining to the nation of Israel. The dualistic nature of this covenant resulted in Abraham having two types of descendants. Spilsbury said, "There was in Abraham at that time a spiritual seed and a fleshly seed. Between which seeds God ever distinguished through all their Generations." Abraham's physical descendants received physical circumcision and the promise of the land; Abraham's spiritual descendants received spiritual circumcision and the promise of a better country in heaven. This principle of physical descendants, they claimed, was limited to national Israel and did not continue into the new covenant.

New Covenant

Puritan Baptists typically saw the new covenant not simply as another administration or new outward expression of the one covenant of grace but as the fulfilment of the promise—the covenant of grace itself, fully revealed and established. The Second London Baptist Confession speaks of the covenant of grace as "revealed in the gospel; first of all to Adam in the promise of salvation by the seed of the woman, and afterwards by farther steps, until the full discovery thereof was completed in the New Testament." Christ, by his perfect accomplishment of redemption, fulfilled all that was promised in the covenant of grace beginning in Genesis 3:15. They taught that the new covenant consisted only of those who were truly regenerate. Thus baptism, being the sign of the covenant, ought only to be administered to those who profess and evidence true saving faith.

Unity Sought

Though there were strong and significant disagreements between both parties, Puritan-minded Baptists and paedobaptists, in their best moments, pursued unity with one another. In his preface to *A Discourse of the Covenants*, Nehemiah Coxe, specifically addressing his paedobaptist brothers against whom he was writing, affirmed, "There is nothing that my soul more longs for on earth than to see an entire and hearty union of all that fear God and hold the Head, however differing in their sentiments about some things of lesser moment." In a similar spirit, the appendix to the Second London Baptist Confession states concerning paedobaptists, "For it is our duty and concern so far as possible for us (retaining a good conscience towards God) to seek a more entire agreement and reconciliation with them."

Reflect

1. What do you find in the argumentation of the Particular Baptists that is biblically compelling? What are some weaknesses?

2. Read Jeremiah 31:31–34. What are the marks of those in the new covenant? Does your life evidence these characteristics?

3. Many of the early Baptists were exemplary in their pursuit of unity with their paedobaptist brothers. How can you hold firmly to your own convictions while still maintaining a proper measure of unity with those who disagree with you about "some things of lesser moment"? What does the promotion of discord within the church reveal about the heart?

Discuss

1. Why does the baptism debate hinge upon one's understanding of the relationship between the covenants God made in redemptive history? How does covenant theology relate to the sacrament of baptism?

2. What does Ephesians 2:12 teach us about the nature and relationship of the various covenants revealed in Scripture?

3. Were the Particular Baptists correct in their belief that the new covenant encompasses only the regenerate? Provide biblical support for your answer.

4. Read 1 Corinthians 1:10. How are we to carry out this mandate when there are strong doctrinal disagreements among us? What can we learn from the Puritans here?

Read

Primary Sources

The 1677/1689 (Second London) Baptist Confession of Faith (especially the chapters concerning salvation [including chapter 7, "Of God's Covenant"] plus the introductory letter, "To the Judicious and Impartial Reader," and the explanatory addendum, "An Appendix"). It can be found, with other critical documents, in Renihan, James, ed., *Faith and Life for Baptists: The Documents of the London Particular Baptist General Assemblies, 1689–1694*. Palmdale, CA: Reformed Baptist Academic Press, 2016.

Coxe, Nehemiah and John Owen. *Covenant Theology: From Adam to Christ*. Palmdale, CA: Reformed Baptist Academic Press, 2005.

Secondary Sources

Renihan, Samuel D. From *Shadow to Substance: The Federal Theology of the English Particular Baptists (1642–1704)*. Oxford: Centre for Baptist History and Heritage, 2018.

Denault, Pascal. *The Distinctiveness of Baptist Covenant Theology: A Comparison between Seventeenth-Century Particular Baptist and Paedobaptist Federalism (Revised Edition)*. Birmingham: Solid Ground Christian Books, 2017.

PART FOUR

Puritan Legacy

Practical Conclusions

Lesson Given by Joel Beeke

Meditate

The Christian life, according to Richard Baxter, consists of "nothing else but the habitual and predominant devotion and dedication of soul, and body, and life, and all that we have to God; and esteeming, and loving, and serving, and seeking Him, before all the pleasures and prosperity of the flesh." Meditate on Romans 12:1.

Learn

It is not enough to merely listen to these lessons on the Puritans. A stirring of interest in the Puritans is not the same thing as a revival of Puritanism. We need the inward disposition of the Puritans—the authentic, biblical, intelligent piety they possessed in our hearts, lives, and churches. Below are ten lessons we learn from them which beckon us onto the path of godliness.

Fill Your Mind with the Bible

Baxter exhorted his people to "love, reverence, read, study, obey and stick close to the Scripture." The Puritans were men of the Book, and they bid us to be the same. They would have us not only fill our minds with general truths about God, but as Henry Lukin writes, "In reading any command or prohibition in Scripture we must make particular application of it to ourselves, as if God had directed it to us in particular or had spoken to us by name or sent a special message from heaven to us."

Embrace Both God's Sovereignty and Human Responsibility

Nearly all of the Puritans taught that God is fully sovereign and man is fully responsible. How that can be resolved logically is beyond our finite minds. But is this not the case whenever we speak about God in His relation to creation? The Puritans call us to strive for a vibrant, experiential Christianity that believingly rests in God's sovereignty and actively owns our God-given duty.

Keep Your Eyes on Jesus Christ

Thomas Brooks wrote, "They do not love Christ who love anything more than Christ.... Miss Christ and you miss all." The Puritans teach us that the Christian life is one of loving infatuation and fascination with the Person of Christ. "If I were to go to heaven, and find that Christ was not there," said Thomas Goodwin, "I would leave immediately, for heaven would be hell to me without Christ."

Love the True God

The Puritans challenge us to grow in our knowledge of the triune God, to see Him that we might lovingly worship, serve, and adore Him. John Owen wrote, "There was no more glorious mystery brought to light in and by Jesus Christ than that of the holy Trinity.... And this revelation is made unto us, not that our minds might be possessed with the notions of it, but that we may know aright how to place our trust in him, how to obey him and live unto him, how to obtain and exercise communion with him, until we come to the enjoyment of him."

Keep Following Christ through Trials

We learn from the Puritans to view God's rod of affliction as His means to write Christ's image more fully upon us so that we may be partakers of His righteousness and holiness. George Swinnock quaintly said, "A sanctified person, like a silver bell, the harder he is smitten, the better he sounds."

Make Your Family a Little Church

The Puritans loved to speak of the family as a church. Baxter said that "a Christian family...is a church, a society of Christians combined for the better worshipping and serving God." Similarly, William Perkins wrote, "These families wherein this service of God is performed are, as it were, little churches, yea even a kind of Paradise upon earth." They encourage us to view family worship not as a dutiful burden but as a joyous delight—a taste of heaven on earth.

Pray Often, Especially for the Holy Spirit

At the conclusion of his treatise on prayer, John Bunyan expressed his desire that "Christians...pray for the Spirit, that is, for more of it, though God hath endued them with it already." We learn from the Puritans what lives of prayerful dependence upon God look like. They teach us to look away from ourselves to the Spirit who alone can empower us to war against the world, the flesh, and the devil, that we might live for God's glory.

Seek Good Christian Friends

Christian friendship was not optional for the Puritans, but an essential means of persevering and growing in grace. William Ames defined the church as "a society of believers joined together in a special bond for the continual exercise of the communion of the saints among themselves." Thomas Watson exhorted, "Associate with sanctified persons; they may, by their counsel, prayers, and holy example, be a means to make you holy. As the communion of saints is in our creed, so it should be our company."

Pray for Your Church and Be Active in Her Worship

The Puritans stressed the tremendous blessing of gathering with God's people to worship Him. David Clarkson said, "The most wonderful things that are now done on earth are wrought in the public ordinances." Matthew Henry added, "How lovely is the sanctuary in the eyes of those who are truly sanctified!" If you would be a healthy Christian, you must give yourself prayerfully and sacrificially to your local congregation.

Be a Serious, Joyful, and Humble Christian

For the Puritans, the Christian life is one in which the deepest solemnity is wed to heavenly delight. How one lives this earthly life has eternal ramifications. John Trapp said, "Piety shall have riches without rust, wealth without want, store without sore, beauty without blemish, mirth without mixture." Being the recipients of such an eternal inheritance in Christ, our lives ought to be characterized by a profound seriousness, joy, and humility.

Reflect

---

1. Of these ten lessons learned from the Puritans, which one do you find yourself most in need of learning? How could you pursue growth in this area over the next year?

2. How formative is the Bible upon your thinking, feeling, and living? Do you exercise a similar devotion to the Scriptures as was manifested in the Puritans?

3. The Puritans struck a healthy balance between the individual and corporate dimensions of the Christian life, teaching the necessity of both personal piety and corporate worship and fellowship. Are you more prone to neglect the individual aspects of Christianity or the corporate? Why is this?

Discuss

1. If you had to summarize these ten lessons into one sentence, what would it be? In other words, what is the overarching, dominating lesson of Puritanism?

2. How do the Puritans integrate the individual soul, the family, and the church? What is the unifying principle that binds them all together?

3. What are the chief characteristics of God-honoring, Christ-exalting friendship? How can this be pursued and cultivated?

4. How can exuberant joy and grave seriousness be wed together in the soul? Why should the Christian life be one of serious joy and joyful seriousness?

Read

Beeke, Joel and Mark Jones. *A Puritan Theology: Doctrine for Life*. Grand Rapids: Reformation Heritage Books, 2012.

Packer, J.I. *A Quest for Godliness: The Puritan Vision of the Christian Life*. Wheaton, IL: Crossway, 1990.

Ryken, Leland. *Worldly Saints: The Puritans as They Really Were*. Grand Rapids: Zondervan, 1986.

Beeke, Joel and Randall Pederson. *Meet the Puritans: With a Guide to Modern Reprints*. Grand Rapids: Reformation Heritage Books, 2006.

About the Authors

JOEL BEEKE is president and professor of systematic theology at Puritan Reformed Theological Seminary and a pastor of Heritage Reformed Congregation, in Grand Rapids, Michigan. He is a leading expert on Puritanism, a frequent conference speaker, and the author of numerous books.

NICHOLAS THOMPSON is an MDiv student at Puritan Reformed Theological Seminary, preparing to minister in the Orthodox Presbyterian Church.

About the Lecturers

BRIAN COSBY is pastor of Wayside Presbyterian Church in Signal Mountain, Tennessee, and adjunct professor of church history at Metro Atlanta Seminary.

MARK DEVER is senior pastor of Capitol Hill Baptist Church in Washington, DC, and president of 9Marks.

SINCLAIR FERGUSON is professor of systematic theology at Reformed Theological Seminary and a teaching fellow of Ligonier Ministries.

IAN HAMILTON is professor of church history at Edinburgh Seminary and president of the Board of Trustees for Banner of Truth Trust.

MICHAEL HAYKIN is professor of church history and biblical spirituality at Southern Baptist Theological Seminary in Louisville, Kentucky.

MARK JONES is pastor of Faith Vancouver Presbyterian Church in British Columbia, Canada, and research associate at the University of the Free State in South Africa.

JAMES LA BELLE is pastor of the Presbyterian Church of Cape Cod, Massachusetts.

JASON MEYER is pastor for preaching and vision of Bethlehem Baptist Church in Minneapolis, Minnesota, and associate professor of New Testament at Bethlehem College & Seminary.

DAVID MURRAY is professor of Old Testament and practical theology at Puritan Reformed Theological Seminary in Grand Rapids, Michigan.

STEPHEN NICHOLS is president of Reformation Bible College and a teaching fellow of Ligonier Ministries.

J. I. PACKER is emeritus professor of theology at Regent College in Vancouver, British Columbia.

JOE RIGNEY is assistant professor of theology and Christian worldview at Bethlehem College and Seminary in Minneapolis, Minnesota.

LELAND RYKEN is emeritus professor of English at Wheaton College in Wheaton, Illinois.

GREG SALAZAR is assistant professor of historical theology at Puritan Reformed Theological Seminary in Grand Rapids, Michigan.

JOHN SNYDER is pastor of Christ Church in New Albany, Mississippi.

DEREK THOMAS is senior minister of First Presbyterian Church in Columbia, South Carolina, and a teaching fellow of Ligonier Ministries.

GEOFF THOMAS served for half a century as a minister of Alfred Place Baptist Church in Aberystwyth, Wales, and is visiting professor of historical theology at Puritan Reformed Theological Seminary in Grand Rapids, Michigan.

CHAD VAN DIXHOORN is professor of church history at Westminster Theological Seminary in Glenside, Pennsylvania.

WILLIAM VANDOODEWAARD is professor of church history at Puritan Reformed Theological Seminary in Grand Rapids, Michigan.

JEREMY WALKER is pastor of Maidenbowere Baptist Church in Crawley, England.

J. STEPHEN YUILLE is the vice president of academics at Heritage College and Seminary, Cambridge, Ontario. He also serves as associate professor of biblical spirituality at The Southern Baptist Theological Seminary, Louisville, Kentucky.